AS/A-LEVEL

Religious Studies

Gordon Reid

ESSENTIAL WORD
DICTIONARY

Philip Allan Updates
Market Place
Deddington
Oxfordshire
OX15 0SE

Tel: 01869 338652
Fax: 01869 337590
e-mail: sales@philipallan.co.uk
www.philipallan.co.uk

ISBN 0 86003 373 2

Acknowledgements
My thanks go to all those people who helped in the preparation of this
dictionary. In particular, special thanks goes to Sarah Tyler for her considerable
assistance and wise counsel; to Arthur Giles, Chief Examiner for Religious
Studies at Edexcel; to Helen Roderick, Principal Examiner; and to Dr Colin
Niven. Above all, thanks to my wife, Alison, and my children, Louise and
Chris, for their love and support.

Printed by Raithby, Lawrence & Co Ltd, Leicester

Introduction

This is a dictionary of all the key terms that you will need to make a success of religious studies at AS/A-level. To help you to put them into their proper context, alongside every term is an abbreviation to show you which religious studies topic this word fits into best — for instance, a term such as **'Abraham (OT/J)'** suggests that Abraham fits best into the topics of the Old Testament and Judaism, whereas **'abortion (P/E)'** fits into Philosophy and Ethics.

The full list of abbreviations is:

OT — Old Testament
NT — New Testament

P — Philosophy
E — Ethics

B — Buddhism
C — Christianity
H — Hinduism
I — Islam
J — Judaism
S — Sikhism

You will find four types of term used in this book:

1 **Key religious personalities** — figures such as Buddha, Jesus, Moses and Muhammad. Under each name there is a short account of the person's life and the reason for their importance.
2 **Religious terms** — dealing with doctrine, dogma and teachings. The meaning of each term is given, often with examples, together with comments from the religious figures and scholars associated with them and a brief discussion on the issues and controversies that may have arisen from them.
3 **Ethical and moral teachings** — covering a wide range of religious and social areas. Here, guidance is given on what the issues are, the controversies which arise from them and a brief insight into how these issues are treated in specific religious traditions.
4 **Philosophical concepts** — looking at the definition of philosophical terms and the debates which centre around their meaning and their implications both for secular society and for religious believers. The names and works of principal scholars are included.

Throughout this book you will find special tips which will offer you simple advice on how to avoid common misunderstandings and guidance on how to make the best use of key terms in the final examinations.

Finally, in many definitions you will find words in italics. This means that these words are defined more fully elsewhere in the dictionary.

Abbreviations for books of the Bible (New International Version)

In this dictionary, several books of the Bible have been abbreviated in the bracketed biblical references. The abbreviations used are as follows:

Old Testament

Gen. — Genesis
Exod. — Exodus
Lev. — Leviticus
Num. — Numbers
Deut. — Deuteronomy
Josh. — Joshua
1 or 2 Sam. — 1 or 2 Samuel
1 or 2 Kgs — 1 or 2 Kings
Ps. — Psalms
Eccles. — Ecclesiastes
Is. — Isaiah
Jer. — Jeremiah
Ezek. — Ezekiel
Dan. — Daniel
Hos. — Hosea

New Testament

Matt. — Matthew
Mk — Mark
Lk — Luke
Jn — John
Rom. — Romans
1 or 2 Cor. — 1 or 2 Corinthians
Gal. — Galatians
Eph. — Ephesians
Phil. — Philippians
1 or 2 Thess. — 1 or 2 Thessalonians
1 or 2 Tim. — 1 or 2 Timothy
Heb. — Hebrews
Rev. — Revelation

References and further reading

The themes in this dictionary can be followed up in a wide range of books and commentaries. In compiling this work, I found the following to be particularly helpful.

Anderson, B. (1996) *The Living World of the New Testament*, Darton, Longman, Todd.
Browning, W. (1996) *A Dictionary of the Bible*, Oxford University Press.
Close, B. (1991) *Judaism*, Hodder & Stoughton.
Cush, D. (1994) *Buddhism*, Hodder & Stoughton.
Davies, B. (1995) *An Introduction to the Philosophy of Religion*, Cambridge University Press.
Drane, J. (1987) *Introducing the Old Testament*, Lion.
Drane, J. (1999) *Introducing the New Testament*, Lion.
Hinnells, J. (ed.) (1995) *The Penguin Dictionary of Religions*, Penguin.

Kee, H. and Young, F. (1996) *The Living World of the New Testament*, Darton, Longman, Todd.

Livingstone, E. (ed.) (1992) *The Concise Oxford Dictionary of the Christian Church*, Oxford University Press.

Mautner, T. (ed.) (1999) *The Penguin Dictionary of Philosophy*, Penguin.

McGrath, A. E. (1994) *Christian Theology: An Introduction*, Blackwell.

Richards, C. (ed.) (1997) *The Illustrated Encyclopedia of World Religions*, Element.

Sen, K. (1991) *Hinduism*, Penguin.

Smart, N. (1992) *The World's Religions*, Cambridge University Press.

Thompson, M. (1992) *Ethics*, Hodder & Stoughton.

Tyler, S. (1998) *Religious Studies: The Philosophy of Religion*, Philip Allan Updates.

Waines, D. (1995) *An Introduction to Islam*, Cambridge University Press.

(1992) *The Holy Bible: New International Version*, Hodder & Stoughton.

Aaron (OT/J): elder brother of Moses.

He spoke for Moses to the Pharaoh (Exod. 4), and supported Moses during the escape from Egypt but gave in to the people's demands and made them a Golden Calf to worship at Mt Sinai (Exod. 32:1–4).

He is most important in his priestly role and was the first *High Priest* of Israel with responsibility for the wilderness *tabernacle*, a special tent used for worship. He died before the Israelites entered Canaan (Num. 20:28) and his son Eleazar became High Priest after him. The priesthood of Israel became known as the 'sons of Aaron'.

Abba (NT): Aramaic word for 'father', a term used for God.

Jesus was the first to apply the term to God in prayer in Gethsemane (Mk 14:36) and gave authority to his disciples to do so. It is a term that conveys a sense of warm intimacy and respect, used by a child to his/her father or as a style of address to a rabbi. However, Jesus' use of the term in prayer was unusual because it was not used in Jewish circles as a form of address to God. Paul refers to the term twice in his letters (Rom. 8:15 and Gal. 4:6). He seems to see the term as a symbol of the Christian's adoption as a child of God.

TIP It is a common mistake to assume that this word was equivalent to the children's word 'Daddy'. This is not so and was more likely to have been used as a type of adult address — a more formal 'father'.

abortion (P/E): termination of a pregnancy.

The term 'natural abortion' is used when referring to a miscarriage; 'clinical abortion' when talking of the termination of a pregnancy by medical techniques. In the UK abortion is governed by the Abortion Act 1967, under which an abortion is permitted if two doctors agree that there is a risk to the life or health of the mother or child if the pregnancy is continued, or if the child would suffer from severe handicap. This is a controversial area, largely condemned by Christian moralists and the Catholic Church.

TIP This is a very popular area of study in essays and coursework. Keep an eye on the newspapers, since views on abortion and improvements in medical science change the arguments very rapidly.

Abraham (also known as 'Abram') **(OT/J/I):** first of the *Patriarchs* of Israel.

■ His life is taken as a shining example of outstanding faith in God, and is described in Genesis 11–25. He was born in Ur around 1700 BCE and was a wealthy man. When he is 75 God tells him to take his family and possessions to the land of Canaan. God promises the new land to him and tells him that he would be 'a great nation'. As Abram, he is granted a unique *covenant* with God, confirming that he will be 'the father of many nations'. The covenant is marked by changing his name to Abraham (meaning 'father of many') and by *circumcision*. His story contains many incidents: he rescues his nephew Lot, who has been taken from Sodom by a group of 'kings'; he travels to Egypt and deceives the king; and he has an illegitimate son, Ishmael, by his wife's servant, Hagar. When he is 100, his wife, Sarah, gives birth to a son, Isaac, and Abraham's faith is later tested when he is asked by God to sacrifice the boy. When Abraham shows his willingness to do so, a ram is substituted by God and Abraham is rewarded by a renewal of God's promise.

In Judaism, Abraham is seen as a great man of God and the recipient of the divine covenant, and the people of Israel were considered to be 'the seed of Abraham'.

In Islam, Abraham (or 'Ibrahim') is one of the most important of the former prophets in the Qur'an. He is regarded as the rebuilder of the *Ka'ba* in Mecca and the propagator of the original *monotheism* later perfected by Muhammad.

■ *TIP* Examination questions on Abraham usually centre on his faith in God. Watch also for questions where the emphasis is not so much on Abraham himself, but on the social and cultural life of patriarchal times.

absolutism (E): term meaning either (1) a system of government in which the ruler's power is not subject to the limitations of a constitution; or (2) an ethical point of view which suggests that there may be certain moral rules that have no exceptions to them.

■ An example of this would be the *Ten Commandments* in Judaism/Christianity. For instance, 'You shall not commit murder' (Exod. 20:13).

Acts of the Apostles (NT): fifth book of the New Testament, generally accepted to be the work of Luke and probably dating from between 70 and 85 CE.

■ It tells of the development of the early Church in the years immediately following the mission of Christ and is the story of the 'acts' (mainly) of the Apostles Peter and Paul. It describes how the followers of Jesus took the Gospel from Jerusalem, the capital of the Jewish world, to Rome itself. It covers the development of the early Church in the face of hostility, emphasises the work of the Holy Spirit, the divine origin of Christianity and the affirmation of the *Resurrection* of Christ. It includes the taking of Jesus' message to the *Gentiles* through Paul's missionary journeys and the beginnings of the early Christian rites of baptism and the *Eucharist.*

act utilitarianism (E): theory of Jeremy *Bentham* whose 'principle of utility' was that all actions should produce the 'greatest happiness for the greatest number'.

▓ According to act utilitarianism, it is the value of the consequences of the particular act that count when deciding whether or not the action is right. As Bentham said: 'For those affected by an action, that action is right if it brings pleasure and wrong if it brings pain.' The theory has been criticised for being too permissive and even for justifying types of crime — for instance, the 'pleasure' a gang of muggers may get from robbing an old lady. A further criticism is that it may be impossible to predict the consequences of any actions and therefore to assess their value.

▓ *TIP* A very popular area for examiners — make sure that you are familiar with the utilitarian theories of Jeremy *Bentham* and John Stuart *Mill*.

Adam (Hebrew word for 'man'/'humanity') **(OT/NT):** name of the first human, according to Genesis.

▓ Adam was created with Eve in the image of God and, unlike the animals, had a personal relationship with God. The disobedience of Adam and Eve led to the '*Fall* of man' (Gen. 1–3). In the New Testament, Adam is regarded as a historical person and Luke's Gospel traces Jesus back to Adam (Lk 3:23–38). Paul contrasts the 'first Adam' of Genesis, who was disobedient before God, to Jesus Christ, the 'second Adam', who was obedient.

Adi Granth (S): 'First Book' and principal scripture of Sikhism.

▓ Compiled in 1603–04 by Arjan, the fifth *Guru*, the scripture contains a message of spiritual liberation through belief in the divine name.

▓ *TIP* This work is now more commonly referred to in textbooks as the '*Guru Granth Sahib*' or 'Revered Book'.

adultery (OT/NT): referred to in the Old Testament as a man having sex with a married woman or a betrothed virgin.

▓ Adultery was prohibited under the *Ten Commandments* (Exod. 20:14), and the penalty for it was death. In the New Testament, Jesus suggests that adultery may be committed by looking at a woman 'lustfully' (Matt. 5:28). In John 8:1–11 there is a story, not universally considered genuine, in which Jesus saves a woman charged with adultery from being stoned to death.

Advent (from the Latin *adventus*, meaning 'coming') **(C):** season which starts the Christian calendar.

▓ In the West, Advent begins on the Sunday nearest to 30 November and lasts until 24 December. It marks the preparation for Christmas and the coming of Jesus Christ into the world. It also looks ahead to the *Second Coming* of Christ on the Last Day.

a fortiori (P): Latin expression, commonly used in philosophy, meaning 'for a stronger reason' or 'all the more'.

agape (NT/C): Greek word meaning 'love'.

▓ 'Agape' is used in the New Testament to describe the self-giving love of God shown in Christ and, correspondingly, of the love of Christians for one another (1 Cor. 13:13). The word also came to be used for the shared meal held by Christians in conjunction with the *Eucharist*.

a

agnosticism (from Greek, meaning 'without knowledge') **(P):** theory according to which only material things can be really known — the spiritual and supernatural realms are unknowable.

▥ Agnostics claim that they do not know, or that it is not possible to know, whether or not God exists. The term was first used by Thomas Huxley in 'Collected Essays' in 1869.

ahimsa **(H/B):** term in Hinduism and Buddhism meaning 'non-harming' or 'non-violence'.

▥ In Hinduism the practice of ahimsa started principally with the rejection of animal sacrifice and the widespread adoption of vegetarianism. Mainly through the influence of Gandhi, complete abstention of all violence is now seen as the ideal for all Hindus.

In Buddhism, the non-harming of living creatures is one of the five 'bases of training' for ethical conduct.

Akal Purakh **(S):** term meaning 'the Eternal One' used in Sikhism by *Guru Nanak* to refer to God.

▥ In the ultimate sense, God is unknowable, but is revealed through the Guru. Nanak spoke of the unity and creating power of God, whose presence is visible to the enlightened believer.

akhira **(I):** the afterlife in Islam.

▥ After the last judgement, the righteous will enter Paradise, which is referred to in the Qur'an as a garden full of delights and the vision of God. The non-righteous, or damned, will enter hell, a place of fire under the control of Malik, the keeper of hell and the demons.

There is some discussion within Islam emphasising the spiritual bliss of Paradise and questioning whether or not going to hell is permanent or for a fixed time only.

akhlaq **(I):** Islamic term for ethics.

▥ It is used to refer to moral and religious virtues, usually emphasising personal responsibility and morality.

alienation **(E):** term meaning the giving over of something that is yours to another party.

▥ Not to be confused with the giving of a gift, the term signifies that the giving over is undesirable or unwelcome. In terms of religion, *Feuerbach* suggested that human beings have failed to see that human nature is good and have given over the human qualities which are actually good to an imaginary God, who is then seen as being loving, kind and so on. Through this alienation, humans come to see themselves as being worthless. For Feuerbach, once people gain an insight into the positive nature of humanity, then their alienation and sense of worthlessness will come to an end.

▥ *TIP* 'Alienation' crops up in examination questions concerning the arguments for the non-existence of God and may be seen in the writings of both Feuerbach and Karl Marx.

Allah (I): name for God in Islam, whom Muhammad proclaimed as the one, unique God.

▨ God is the creator of all things, the controller of nature and the sovereign lord of all. He will judge humanity in the last days.

Many Muslims use the 'ninety-nine most beautiful names' ('al-asma al-husna') given to Allah for liturgical and devotional purposes. The names describe the attributes of Allah, such as the Creator, the Sustainer, the Most Compassionate and the Most Merciful.

Unity and oneness of God is of great importance in Islam, and polytheism (the worship of many gods) is the supreme, unforgivable sin.

Alleluia (also spelt 'Hallelujah') **(OT/NT):** term meaning 'Praise the Lord'.

▨ It is found in the Psalms and Revelation 19:1, and became incorporated into Christian worship.

alms (OT/NT): giving of aid to the poor.

▨ In the Old Testament, people were encouraged to show compassion for the needy (Deut. 15:7–8; Psalm 41:1). In the synagogues there was an organised system to help the poor and in the *Temple* there were six receptacles in the shape of trumpets, into which people could put alms.

In the New Testament, Jesus encouraged people to give alms in secret and condemned those who made a show of it (Matt. 6:1–4; Mk 12:41–44).

In the early Church, *deacons* were appointed to administer alms to the poor (Acts 6:1–7) and Paul asked churches to set up a proper system of almsgiving to the poor Christians in Jerusalem.

altar (OT/NT/C): in the Bible, a place where animals were sacrificed and where gifts of corn, wine and incense were burned and offered to God.

▨ Altars were places of extreme holiness and could be made of earth, stone or metal. They were also used by individuals to pray to God or to seek refuge from their enemies (1 Kgs 2:39). The term later became used to refer to the Eucharistic Table, from which the *Eucharist* was celebrated. The earliest such altars were probably wooden tables, although sometimes Eucharist was celebrated on 'stone altars', which were the tombstones of Christian martyrs. In the Christian Church, the altar is the centrepiece of worship.

altruism (E): ethical term meaning a benevolent concern for the interests and welfare of others.

▨ The term was first used by the French philosopher Auguste Comte (1798–1857). The notion of altruism has caused much controversy. Several moralists have suggested that altruism is merely used by people to disguise their own self-interest; others, such as *Hume* and Butler, have said that altruism is nothing more than a subtle way for people to satisfy their own desires and interests.

Amen (from the Hebrew word meaning 'certainly') **(NT/C):** term commonly said at the end of prayers.

▨ Jesus is sometimes himself referred to as 'the Amen', and 'Amen' is the last word in the Bible.

a

amidah (J): the central prayer of the Jewish *liturgy*.

▨ The word *amidah* literally means 'standing', since the prayer is said standing and facing *Jerusalem*. It consists of 19 benedictions (prayer for divine blessing) and is recited three times a day and in a slightly different form on the *Sabbath*.

amoral (E): term meaning having no moral awareness or moral concerns.

▨ The term was originated by the French philosopher Jean Guyau (1854–88).

Amos (OT): prophet from Judah.

▨ Amos spoke out against the evils he saw in *Israel* during the reign of Jeroboam II (786–746 BCE). He was angered by the luxurious living of the rich (Amos 3:15) and the injustice against the poor and foresaw God's judgement against the land (Amos 6:11).

The Book of Amos follows the theme that God is the universal God of all nations, upon whom he makes moral demands. He has a special relationship with Israel but, Amos warns, the nation would not be saved by empty religious rituals (Amos 5:21–22). Judgement would come, but Amos kept alive the hope of eventual restoration (Amos 9:11–15).

In the New Testament, Amos is quoted by Stephen (Acts 7:43) and by James (Acts 15:16).

▨ *TIP* This is a very popular topic with examiners — make sure that you understand Amos' message, including his five visions and the teachings on the *day of the Lord* and the hope for the future. Examination questions often centre around Amos' teaching on moral and social righteousness.

Anabaptists (C): refers to a number of sixteenth-century religious groups which rejected infant *baptism*, believing instead in the baptism of mature believers as a mark of church membership.

▨ The main Anabaptist groups were (1) Munzer and the Zwickau Prophets; (2) the Swiss Brethren; (3) communities in Moravia under the leadership of Hutter; (4) Hoffmanites or Melchiorites; (5) Munster Anabaptists; (6) the Mennonites. The Anabaptists were denounced by *Calvin, Luther* and *Zwingli*, and persecuted by both Catholics and Protestants.

anagarika (B): Buddhist term (meaning 'non-householder') for a person who has left their home in order to search for the truth about life.

▨ The Buddha himself left his home and family to find enlightenment, and the practice stems from the earliest days of Buddhism and is regarded as a very honourable thing to do. The person may become a homeless traveller, depending on the goodwill of others for their sustenance.

analogy (P): term meaning 'similarity' or 'likeness', used in religious language when attempting to explain how religious statements make sense.

▨ If we use ordinary words to try to describe God, then we reduce God to human levels. However, an analogy can be used to make a comparison to show how two qualities, one human and one divine, are similar, and thus we are able to understand God better. For instance, if I say 'I love my children' and then we say 'God loves everyone', then my love is analogous to God's love, even though

God's love is different from human love. The doctrine of analogy is associated with St Thomas *Aquinas*.

analytic statement (P): where a word or statement has its full meaning contained within it.

'Bachelor' is an example of an analytic 'statement', because it says exactly what an unmarried male is. So, when talking about someone, if we say that they are a 'bachelor', then we automatically know that they are male and unmarried, since 'male' and 'unmarried' are contained within the meaning of the word 'bachelor'. In religious language, philosophers debate the issue of whether or not the word 'God' is analytic, and argue whether we need to have a further explanation and definition to understand exactly what we mean by God.

anarchism (E): theory or political movement in which all relationships of power and domination are rejected.

In particular, anarchism rejects as unjust those political structures and states in which there are rulers and subjects. Instead, it advocates social organisation based on small autonomous communities in which individuals work together towards a common purpose. The term was first used by William Godwin in his work 'An Enquiry Concerning the Principles of Political Justice', 1793.

anatta (B): Buddhist term (meaning 'not self'), one of the 'three marks' of all conditioned existence, along with *anicca* and *dukkha*.

In Buddhism, if a person believes they have an eternal, unchanging 'self', it leads them into a distorted view of life and therefore causes them to suffer. To be free of this they must understand that there is no 'self'. This is the basis of Buddhist ethics — as long as a person is restricted by the notion of 'self', then they cannot really act selflessly for the benefit of others.

angel (OT/NT): from the Greek term *aggelos*, meaning 'messenger'.

Angels are depicted in the Bible as supernatural beings who form the 'heavenly host' or heavenly court (Is. 6:3) and who dwell with God and carry out his commands. Some angels have names, the most famous being the Angel Gabriel. In the New Testament, angels are described as spiritual beings who will be present at the *Second Coming* (Matt. 16:27 and 22:30) and appear with Jesus at various stages throughout his mission (e.g. Matt. 4:11). There are also a number of evil angels under the charge of *Satan* (Matt. 25:41).

In the early Christian Church, Dionysius attempted to arrange the order of angels into three hierarchies of three choirs each; in the first were Seraphim, Cherubim and Thrones, in the second were Dominations, Virtues and Powers and in the third were Principalities, Archangels and Angels.

Anglicanism (C): strictly speaking, a system of doctrine and practice upheld by those Christians in communion with the see of Canterbury; often used today when referring to the established Church of England.

Anglican doctrine was originally expressed partly in the 'Thirty-Nine Articles' of 1563, partly in the *Book of Common Prayer* and partly in the Homilies, which were official sermons given in 1563 and 1571.

a

Anglicanism claims that holy scripture contains all that is necessary for eternal salvation and that truth can be found through the words of scripture and religious authority.

In the Anglican Church, government is through bishops and worship is primarily contained within fixed liturgies. Bishops of the world-wide 'Anglican Communion' meet for regular conference in Lambeth in London.

anicca (meaning 'impermanent') **(B):** Buddhist term, one of the 'three marks' of all conditioned existence, along with *anatta* and *dukkha*.

In Buddhism, all things are said to exist only for a moment — that is, they are impermanent. Some Buddhist schools, such as the Sarvastivada, have tried to calculate the length of the moment, whilst others, like the Sautrantika, have said that impermanence means that change is happening continuously, without stopping even for a moment. Anicca is investigated through *Vipassana* meditation.

Annunciation (NT): message brought to *Mary* by the Angel Gabriel telling her that she had been chosen to be the mother of the Son of God (Lk 1:26–38).

In the Christian Church, the 'Annunciation of the Blessed Virgin Mary' is observed on 25 March ('Lady Day').

anoint (OT/NT): act of consecrating (dedicating) a person or thing to the service of God.

In the Old Testament, kings such as *Solomon* were anointed with oil (1 Kgs 1:39) and priests were anointed for office.

In the New Testament, Jesus was said to be anointed by the *Holy Spirit* (Acts 10:38) and anointing was also used to help the sick and as a sign of affection to the living (Lk 7:37–38) and the dead (Mk 16:1).

The Hebrew word '*Messiah*' refers to the notion of God's 'Anointed One'.

Anselm of Canterbury (1033–1109) (P): Italian-born Archbishop of Canterbury from 1093, who devised the *ontological argument* for the existence of God.

Anselm produced a series of treatises on important problems in theology and philosophy of religion. Unlike other thinkers of his day, he defended his faith not by arguing from the Bible, but by using intellectual reasoning. He is most famous for devising the ontological argument in his work **Proslogion**, in which he said that God is a being greater than which none can be conceived.

TIP The ontological argument is a key part of many Philosophy of Religion examinations and is sometimes used in contrast with the *cosmological* and *teleological arguments*. It is a difficult concept to grasp — make sure that you know the definition and the arguments, both in its favour and against it.

antecedentialism (E): moral theory which suggests that looking back on the circumstances can actually help to determine whether an action is right.

If someone risks their life to save another, for example, the rescuer deserves a reward and therefore it is right to give a reward, even though, at the time of the rescue, the rescuer did not act because he/she was looking for a reward.

TIP In an examination, this may be contrasted with *consequentialism*, which suggests that looking backwards is irrelevant. In the above example, the consequentialist might say that a reward should only be offered if doing so will have beneficial consequences.

anthropomorphic (P): term meaning 'in human likeness' or 'with human characteristics'.

■ Descriptions of God are sometimes anthropomorphic in order to make him understandable — for example, 'God loves us like a father loves his children.'

Antichrist (NT/C): title given in Christianity to the supreme enemy of Christ (2 Thess. 1:3) and the opponents of the Church (1 Jn 2:18).

■ The Antichrist is supposed to appear before the Last Judgement and is a symbol of the revolt against Christ.

anti-Semitism (J): term used to describe antagonism or prejudice against Jews.

■ Active persecution of Jews has been bound up with Christian attitudes towards them through the ages. Jews have been accused of a range of things through the centuries, from being responsible for the death of Jesus ('deicide') to the desecration of the wafer used in the *Eucharist* and the ritual murder of Christian children, whose blood was said to be used to make the unleavened bread eaten at *Passover*. Jews have, since the Middle Ages, been expelled or ill-treated in almost every Christian country in Europe. Anti-Semitism reached its peak during the Nazi Holocaust of 1939–45.

anukampa (B): Buddhist term for 'sympathy'.

■ It refers to the motivation which impels a Buddha and his disciples to teach and give help to the people of the world as a whole.

■ *TIP* In *Mahayana* Buddhism, this term has been superseded by the term 'karuna'.

Apocalypse (OT/NT/C): term meaning an unveiling or revelation of divine secrets, and another name for the Book of Revelation.

■ The term 'apocalypse' is used in the Bible to describe visions and revelations from God concerning the whole range of human experience and beyond, including the events which will occur at the end of time. In the Old Testament, apocalyptic writings can be found in the books of Daniel, *Isaiah* and Zechariah. In the New Testament, Mark 13 is called the 'Little Apocalypse', whilst the most famous example of all is the Book of Revelation.

Apocrypha (from the Greek, meaning 'hidden things') **(C):** the biblical books which were not included in the Hebrew Bible.

■ They date from 300 BCE to 100 CE. The full list is 1 and 2 Esdras, Tobit, Judith, the rest of Esther, the Wisdom of Solomon, Ecclesiasticus, Baruch, Song of the Three Children, History of Susanna, Bel and the Dragon, The Prayer of Manasses, and 1 and 2 Maccabees.

Apodictic Law (OT): type of law in the Old Testament which expresses absolute prohibitions or injunctions.

■ Apodictic Law is easily identified in the *Ten Commandments* and elsewhere, because it usually begins with expressions such as, 'You shall not...'.

a

apologetics (from the Greek *apologia*, meaning 'a defence against criticism') **(P):** branch of theology that deals with the defence of religious beliefs against criticism.

▦ *TIP* Some scholars have suggested that the Gospels, particularly Luke, may be apologetics, defending the early Christians in the face of persecution.

apostasy (OT/NT): repudiation of faith in God.

▦ This is a common theme amongst the Old Testament prophets such as Hosea and Jeremiah, who accuse the people of Israel of turning away from God. In the New Testament, Paul suggests that final judgement will come after the 'apostasy' or 'rebellion' (2 Thess. 3:3).

▦ *TIP* The notion of 'apostasy' is a common theme in many Old Testament questions concerning the prophets, particularly Hosea and Jeremiah.

a posteriori (from the Latin for 'what comes after') **(P):** term used in philosophy to refer to knowledge and truth claims which are based upon, dependent upon or derived from experience.

▦ *TIP* The *cosmological argument* is an 'a posteriori' argument, since it is based upon experience.

Apostle (from the Greek *apostolos*, meaning 'messenger') **(NT):** in the New Testament, name given to the twelve disciples of Christ, who bore witness to the message of Jesus and continued his work.

▦ In Luke 6:14–16, the Apostles are listed as Peter, Andrew, James, John, Philip, Bartholomew, Thomas, Matthew, James, son of Alphaeus, Judas, son of James, Simon the Zealot and, later according to Acts 1:26, Matthias (who replaced Judas Iscariot). The term is also applied in the *Acts of the Apostles* to Paul and Barnabas.

a priori (from the Latin expression 'from what comes earlier') **(P):** term used in philosophy to mean 'without experience' or 'prior to experience', used in theoretical arguments, or arguments based on definitions.

▦ *TIP* The *ontological argument* is an 'a priori' argument, since it is based on definitions, not experience.

Aquida (meaning 'creed') **(I):** Islamic term for the profession of faith in the unity of God and the prophethood of *Muhammad.*

▦ It is used liturgically in Islamic worship.

Aquinas, St Thomas (c. 1225–74) (P): one of the greatest Catholic theologians.

▦ Aquinas attempted to apply the philosophy of Aristotle to Christianity. In his most famous work, **Summa Theologica**, he suggested that God reveals certain truths that cannot be otherwise known, and assists humanity to discover other truths through the use of reason. He is remembered for his 'Five Ways', which were arguments for the existence of God. The first three ways became known as the popular form of the *cosmological argument.*

▦ *TIP* A very important philosopher — look for him particularly in questions concerning the existence of God, miracles and religious language.

Arahat (B): Buddhist term for someone who has achieved enlightenment by fully realising the *Four Noble Truths* and becoming free of all forms of attachment and delusion. The Arahat is released from the cycle of rebirth and will not be reborn.

■ *TIP* There is some controversy amongst Buddhists. *Mahayana* criticism had suggested that the path to becoming an Arahat is ruled by a selfish concern for one's own release and is, therefore, inferior to the path of the *Bodhisattva*, which is based more on becoming a *Buddha* and then bringing release from suffering to others.

ardas (S): petition or formal prayer that ends Sikh rituals.

■ It begins with praise of the Ten *Gurus*, followed by a remembrance of past trials and triumphs, followed by the prayer of petition itself.

argument (P): in philosophy, set of propositions of which one, the end or conclusion, is supposed to follow from what has been said earlier.

Aristotle (384–232 BCE) (P/E): Greek philosopher who, as a young man, was a disciple of Plato.

■ He is famous for a range of philosophical writings, and he dubbed God the 'first unmoved mover'. In his ethical theories, he believed that humans sought happiness and that this could best be achieved if they functioned well, and, in particular, lived life according to reason (***Nicomachean Ethics, Book 1***). He made a distinction between moral and intellectual excellence and claimed that it was natural for humans to live together in societies and to behave morally towards each other.

Ark (OT/NT/J): (1) vessel in which *Noah*, his family and the animals escaped from the Flood (Gen. 6–9); (2) Ark of the Covenant, the most sacred religious symbol of the Hebrews.

■ The Ark of the Covenant was believed to represent the Presence of God. It was a large wooden box, overlaid inside and out with gold, and was said to contain the two tablets on which God had written the Law (Deut. 10:5). The people of Israel carried it with them during the *Exodus* and into the land of Canaan. Later it was placed in the 'Holy of Holies' (inner part of the *tabernacle*) of Solomon's *Temple* in Jerusalem (1 Kgs 8:6). It was claimed that any who desecrated the Ark would die (1 Sam. 6:19), and at the time of Samuel it was captured by the Philistines (1 Sam. 4:11), who suffered so badly as a result that they returned it to Israel. It is believed that the Ark was lost when the Babylonians attacked Jerusalem in 586 BCE.

■ *TIP* The Ark of the Covenant is an important part of Old Testament history and is likely to come in questions concerning Moses and the Exodus, Samuel, Saul, David and Solomon.

artha (H): Hindu term, one of the four 'goals of life' (along with *Kama, dharma* and *moksha*).

■ It refers to those activities which seek to gain and keep material possessions — the world as seen by economists and politicians. The most famous writing on the subject is the 'Artha-shastra', which declares that it is concerned 'primarily with the attainment of the ends irrespective of the nature of the means employed'.

Asalha (B): Buddhist festival which marks the first teaching of the Buddha.

It falls on the full-moon day of the month of Asalha, which roughly corresponds to June/July. It also marks the start of 3 months of 'rains retreat', where certain Buddhist monks choose to remain inside the monasteries and increase their religious activity. And it is a time when laymen may take up a period of temporary ordination.

Ascension (NT/C): the time when Jesus, after the *Resurrection* appearances, finally goes up to heaven.

 The event is recorded in Acts 1:1–11, where Jesus, after speaking his final words to the disciples, is then 'taken up' before their eyes and hidden by a cloud.
Ascension Day is one of the main festivals in Christianity and is kept on the sixth Thursday, which is the fortieth day after Easter.

aseity (from the Latin *aseitas*, meaning 'from oneself') **(P):** philosophical term, used to refer to the ability to have within oneself the ground for one's own existence, depending on nothing else.

 It is used to refer to God, who is said to exist without depending on anything else.

 TIP Humans do not possess such a quality, since we depend on food, air etc. for our existence.

ashrama (H): Hindu term referring to the four stages of life — the pupil, the householder, the hermit and the stage of renunciation of the world.

 Each of the four stages (ashramas) has its own rules of life, or dharma, and, hence, there are four ashrama-dharmas. The four stages represent the ideal way of life.

atheism (meaning 'godless') **(P):** belief that there is no God, or that the notion of God can be explained by reference to some other phenomena.

atman (B/H): controversial Hindu and Buddhist concept meaning 'self'; in the *Upanishads* it came to be used to mean the true or inner self, the innermost nature of every living being.

 In Hinduism, the most common view is that the atman remains pure and unchanging, even when the body undergoes death and rebirth.
In Buddhism, the atman is not seen as unchanging, and many Buddhists prefer the term *anatta*, meaning 'not self'.

atonement (OT/NT/C/J): literally 'at-one-ment', most commonly referring to the way in which humanity is reconciled with God through the death of Jesus Christ.

 In the Old Testament, people would make *sacrifices* and give offerings to God in order to seek his forgiveness for their sins and remove the barrier caused by sin which cuts them off from God's favour — in other words, they are back 'with God'. This is atonement.
In the New Testament, atonement is used in connection with the life, death and Resurrection of Jesus — his 'sacrifice' atones for the sins of humanity (Mk 10:45; Rom. 3:25).
In Judaism, the 'Day of Atonement' (*Yom Kippur*) is a day of rest and fasting to give space for atoning for the sins of the past year.

Augustine, St (354–430 CE) (C/P): one of the great theological and philosophical figures of his age.

■ St Augustine is particularly remembered for his teachings on the *Fall* of humankind, predestination, original sin and the problem of evil and suffering. He taught that God was the creator of all things and that they were 'good'. Evil is the 'going wrong' of that which is good. He said that, due to the Fall, humans suffer from a kind of hereditary moral disease and are subject to the liability caused by Adam's sin. Humanity can be saved from these evils by God's grace. His most famous writings are **Confessions** and **City of God**.

authoritarianism (E): system of decision making where a person or group makes a decision without consulting the parties concerned.

■ An example of authoritarianism is a political system where the elite make the laws without regard for the opinions of those people who are subject to these rules.

authority (OT/NT/E): (1) the right to decide on matters and issues within a given area; (2) important or valuable source of information.

■ An example of the first type of authority would be a head teacher, who has the authority to decide such matters as what time the school opens. The second type could be an expert, for example a doctor who is an authority on heart disease. In the Old Testament, the prophets were said to have been delegated authority by God to speak for him.

In the New Testament, Jesus has God's authority to forgive sins (Mk 2:10) and exercise judgement (Jn 5:27). St Paul also talks of the authority of the State (Rom. 13:1–7).

autocracy (E): in politics, a term meaning absolute rule.

■ It refers to a state under the absolute rule of a leader who is not subject to constitutional limitations.

autonomy (E): in ethics, a person's capacity for self-determination.

■ When a person is able to decide freely for themselves when and how to act in a moral way, regardless of any external considerations, they are said to have autonomy. This was an important concept in *Kant*'s ethical writings, for instance, in **Foundations of the Metaphysics or Morals** (1785).

avatar (from Sanskrit, meaning 'coming down') **(H):** Hindu concept, referring to the *incarnation* of a deity.

■ The term is usually applied in the worship of the deity *Vishnu*, who is said to have come down to earth in either animal or human form to save the world at times of great crisis. Vishnu has appeared in animal form as a fish, a turtle, a boar, a man-lion and in the human forms of a dwarf, Rama-with-the-axe (Parashurama), *Rama*, *Krishna* and the Buddha. One avatar, called Kalkin, is yet to come and will appear at the end of the present age.

Ayatullah (I): Islamic term meaning 'miraculous sign from God', a title given to high dignitaries of the Shi'ite religious hierarchy.

■ The title is given, in particular, to those eminent scholars who are qualified to give authoritative judgements in matters of faith and practice.

a

Ayer, Sir Alfred (1910–89) (P): Professor of Philosophy at London and Oxford.

■ He is perhaps best remembered for his work ***Language, Truth and Logic*** (1936), in which he highlighted the views of the *Vienna Circle* and *logical positivism*. In his version, everything which is capable of being true or false is divided into two categories. The first is that of 'necessarily true propositions', which are mathematical and logical-style statements that are said to be 'true' by virtue of the meaning of the words which express them, e.g. 'one and one make two'. The second are those propositions which are contingently true, that is, scientific and other statements which can be tested by our senses. Underlying all this was the notion that statements could only be true or false (verifiable) if they fell within one of these two categories. Hence religious and moral statements, e.g. 'You should love one another', are neither true nor false, since they do not fall within the categories.

■ *TIP* Ayer's work is very important, and will be particularly useful in questions concerning religious language and meaning. Make sure you understand his arguments concerning the nature of truth and falsehood, particularly as to how they might apply to religious statements.

Baal (Hebrew term meaning 'lord' or 'master') **(OT):** used in the Old Testament as a noun describing the widely worshipped god of fertility and agriculture in the Canaanite religion.

■ A constant theme of the Old Testament is the way that the Israelites, having settled down in Canaan, were often tempted to transfer their religious allegiance away from God, who had led them out of Egypt and through the desert, to a god (such as *Baal*) who could give them good harvests. This is highlighted in 1 Kgs 18:16–40 and 2 Kings 23:4.

baptism (from the Greek, meaning 'to bathe') **(C):** sacramental rite which, for believers, is a public statement of their faith.

■ Baptism is normally done within a special church service, where the person being baptised is either immersed in water or has water poured upon their forehead (affusion), followed by a signing of the Cross. The use of water was common in Jewish purification rituals in biblical times, and its use among the early Christians is therefore understandable. In the New Testament, John the Baptist invited his listeners to be baptised in the River Jordan, and Jesus was himself baptised in this way (Mk 1:9–13). In the early Church, baptism became a rite of initiation. Peter urged his listeners in Jerusalem to be baptised (Acts 2:38) and Philip baptised an Ethiopian official (Acts 8:36–39). Baptism has been seen by many as a symbolic 'washing away' of their sins and a new beginning.

■ *TIP* The exact nature of baptism has always been a source of conflict within the Christian Church (and, therefore, a rich source of examination questions). One long-running argument centres upon whether or not the person being baptised has to have faith, or whether it is possible to baptise babies and young children who cannot answer for themselves.

Baptist (C): member of any of several Protestant and evangelical Christian sects that practise *baptism* by immersion upon profession of faith.

■ Baptists originated in Amsterdam under John Smyth in the early seventeenth century. Smyth believed that the baptism of mature believers only was the mark of church membership. The Baptists have always emphasised the independence of the individual church and can perhaps be best described as a loose family of churches. Baptists in the UK are part of the *World Council of Churches*.

■ *TIP* The Baptists' emphasis on the independence of local churches means that there is a great variety of belief and practice under the broad title of 'Baptist'. Be careful not to make sweeping statements like 'All Baptists believe...'.

Bar/Bat Mitzvah (Hebrew for 'son/daughter of the commandment') (J): Jewish ceremony marking a child's passage into adulthood.

■ Jewish boys are considered to be adults on their thirteenth birthday, and girls on their twelfth, and they are then deemed to be responsible for keeping the commandments.

Barth, Karl (1886–1968) (C/P): Swiss Protestant theologian.

■ Barth believed in the prophetic teachings of the Bible and the principles of the *Reformation*, and taught that God's only means of communication with humanity was through the scriptures and the revelation of Christ. In particular, he opposed modern theological tendencies which sought to use human reason, which, he felt, was of little value compared to the infinite wisdom of God. His most famous work was ***The Epistle to the Romans*** (1919).

Beatific Vision (C): concept in Catholic theology referring to the final end.

■ The Beatific Vision is the timeless, unchanging vision of God that is the ultimate end for all believers.

Beatitude (NT): type of blessing, most commonly used in relation to the opening part of Jesus' *Sermon on the Mount* in Matthew 5:3–12 and in the Sermon on the Plain in Luke 6.

■ The sermons begin with a number of Beatitudes which talk about the arrival of Jesus in the *kingdom of God*. They start 'Blessed are...' and cover a range of people — the poor in spirit, the meek, the merciful and others. They are words of *eschatology* and encouragement for the future. Individual Beatitudes can also be found elsewhere, e.g. in the Psalms and in Acts 20:35.

Benedictus (NT/C): name given to the Song of Thanksgiving given by Zecharias for the birth of John the Baptist (Lk 1:68–79).

■ It is sometimes sung during the Service of Morning Prayer in the Christian Church.

Bentham, Jeremy (1748–1832) (E): philosopher and social reformer.

■ He is most famous for his theory of *utilitarianism*, laid out in his work ***An Introduction to the Principles of Morals and Legislation*** (1789). His 'principle of utility' suggested that an action could be right if it has consequences which lead to happiness, and wrong if it brings about the reverse. Therefore, society should aim for 'the greatest happiness for the greatest number'. This is sometimes called 'The Greatest Happiness Principle' (GHP). According to Bentham, 'good' is that which leads to the greatest amount of pleasure and the smallest amount of pain. A right moral action, therefore, is one that produces the greatest pleasure. Bentham attempted to measure pleasure and pain by means of the 'Hedonic Calculus', which looked at such factors as the duration of the action, its remoteness and its intensity. Utilitarianism has been criticised on a number of grounds, particularly concerning its emphasis on consequences and happiness, which may lead to a lack of justice and human rights.

▨ *TIP* Bentham and utilitarianism are very important parts of all ethics courses. There may be questions on utilitarianism as an ethical theory, and you will need to know its distinctive features and its strengths and weaknesses.

Bethlehem (OT/NT/C): small town in Israel about 8 km (5 miles) from Jerusalem.

▨ It is mentioned in the Old Testament as the birthplace of King David, but is most famous as the birthplace of Jesus Christ (Lk 2:4). The 'Church of the Nativity' now stands on the supposed birthsite.

Bhagavad Gita (H): 'Song of the Blessed One'— verse *Upanishad* included in the *Mahabharata*.

▨ It is an account of the conversation between the hero Arjuna and his charioteer, *Krishna*. On the eve of a battle, Arjuna refuses to fight, and Krishna attempts to persuade him to join the battle, using a range of arguments, from the social (that people would think that he was a coward) to the philosophical (that no one is killed; the self is reincarnated). At the climax, Krishna reveals himself as a deity. The Bhagavad Gita story is taken as a model for the actions which everyone must take in life. It has gained in popularity in recent years through the influence of *Gandhi*.

bhakti (H): activity of devotion to God, and one of the three paths to salvation in Hinduism — the others being ritual activity and spiritual knowledge.

▨ The devotee to God is called a 'Bhakta'. He or she is usually devoted to a particular manifestation of deity, such as *Krishna* or *Rama*, and will usually adhere to a school of devotion.

bhavana (meaning 'bringing into being') **(B):** term referring to Buddhist meditation, pointing towards the last of the *Four Noble Truths*.

▨ Buddhist meditation practice is of two types — calm meditation and insight meditation — and they are usually developed together in order to achieve a higher order of the mind.

Bible (from the Greek *biblia*, meaning 'books') **(OT/NT/C/J):** collection of sacred books of the Jewish and Christian religions, put together under one cover.

▨ The Hebrew or Jewish Bible (which Christians refer to as the 'Old Testament') consists of 24 books (although the Old Testament was arranged into 39 books by the Protestant Church and 43 by the Catholic Church) and has traditionally been divided into three parts — the Law (Torah), the Prophets and the Writings. The New Testament consists of 27 books, including the Four Gospels, the letters of Paul and the Revelation. The first English translation of the Latin Bible was produced in 1380 under the influence of John Wycliff, and in 1525 William Tyndale translated the Greek New Testament. Miles Coverdale's 1539 revision was known as the 'Great Bible', and perhaps the most famous translation of all was the 'Authorised' or 'King James Version' of 1611. More recent translations include the 'Revised Standard Version' and the 'New International Version'.

b

biblical criticism (OT/NT/C): examination of the books of the Bible by use of historical investigation, archaeological evidence and linguistics.

■ The aim is to try to shed light on what the writers of the Bible were saying, given the situation and the way people thought in those days. There are several types of biblical criticism: (1) textual criticism looks towards the text itself, trying to establish how reliable it is and attempting to get as close as possible to the meaning of the original words of the writers; (2) historical criticism looks at the accuracy of the history — authorship, dates and so on; (3) source criticism looks at where the biblical material comes from — it is most commonly used in a study of the Synoptic Gospels (Matthew, Mark, Luke) to investigate whether or not the authors used the same or similar source material in writing their Gospels; (4) form criticism looks at the lifestyle of the time, and examines the 'form' in which the writing and the ideas may have been shaped at the time; (5) redaction criticism looks at the ways in which the authors, particularly of the Gospels, shaped the material they had in particular ways, for instance the use made of material in Mark by the authors of Matthew and Luke.

Bismillah (I): Islamic phrase meaning 'In the name of God, the Merciful, the Compassionate'.

■ The phrase begins all but one of the suras (chapters) of the Qur'an, and is used by Muslims to ask for divine blessing before certain daily or solemn actions.

Black theology (C): Christian theology that emphasises the experiences of black people.

■ Black theology can be traced back to Henry Turner in the nineteenth century and to Marcus Garvey in the mid-twentieth century. It has been claimed that Black theology is the way in which black people might make clearer sense of a world which has treated them as objects of the white man's trade, and can be found most clearly in sermons, folk tales, dance and songs. It came into prominence during the US civil rights movements in the 1960s and 1970s.

blasphemy (OT/NT/C): speech, thought or action which deliberately displays contempt for God and was punishable by death in biblical times (Lev. 24:16).

■ Jesus was accused of blasphemy because he forgave sins, which only God could do (Matt. 9:1–3), and his claim to having a unique relationship with God led the *Sanhedrin* to find Jesus guilty of blasphemy (Mk 14:61–64). Blasphemy was regarded by the Catholic Church as a mortal sin when aimed against God, the Church or the saints.

blessing (OT/NT/C): (1) words praising God; (2) words used to make something or someone holy by pronouncing God's favour upon them.

■ In the Old Testament, a blessing was a favour given by God, such as a good harvest (Deut. 28:2–3). In the New Testament, blessings are more spiritual, usually referring to gifts promised by God to humanity through Christ. In the Christian Church, a prayer of blessing is often made during the *liturgy*, for example the blessing of the bread and wine in the *Eucharist* service. In many churches, services are concluded with a blessing given by the priest from the altar.

b

blik (P): term used by R. M. *Hare* to mean a way of looking at the world.

A 'blik' cannot be proved to be true or false, but it is seen to affect the conduct of the person who believes it. The example Hare gave was of a lunatic who thought that dons were trying to kill him — this could not be proved one way or another, but it affected the lunatic's actions.

blood (OT/NT): significant in the Bible.

In the Old Testament, it is referred to as the seat of life and therefore has an important role. It was part of the sacrifice ritual — priests were consecrated with it (Exod. 29:21) and blood was sprinkled on the altar to expiate sins and splashed on the people to establish the *covenant* (Exod. 24:8).

In the New Testament, the blood of Christ signifies the saving power of his death, and this is remembered in the *Communion* Service, echoing Jesus' words in the Last Supper: 'This cup is the new covenant in my blood, which is poured out for you' (Lk 22:20).

Bodhgaya (B): name given to the place of the Buddha's enlightenment.

In Bihar, India, it is one of four main Buddhist sites of pilgrimage (along with Kusinara, Lumbini and Sarnath) and, according to tradition, anyone who visits these sites will be reborn in favourable circumstances. Today, Bodhgaya is a thriving pilgrimage centre.

Bodhisattva (B): title given in Buddhism to someone who has taken a vow to attain perfect Buddhahood and is actually on the path towards it.

The path is very long and begins with the 'Bodhicitta' or 'thought of enlightenment' and then follows through ten levels ('bhumi') and a scheme of five paths ('marga'), involving the gradual attainment of the 'paramita' or 'perfections'. In *Mahayana* Buddhism, Bodhisattvas are said to be always present and actively seeking to help the world.

body of Christ (C): term used in Christianity, for both its literal and its symbolic meaning.

It is used in four different ways: (1) the human body of Christ, which was changed at the *Resurrection*; (2) the Church itself, with Christ as the Head; (3) the consecrated bread used at the *Eucharist*; (4) in Latin, **Corpus Christi**, the feast commemorating the institution of the Eucharist.

Bonhoeffer, Dietrich (1906–45) (C): German Lutheran pastor.

He was head of a seminary of the Confessing Church but was forbidden by the Nazis from teaching and was banned from Berlin. In 1942 he tried to form a link between the British government and those Germans who were opposed to Hitler and the Nazis. He was imprisoned in 1943 and executed in 1945. His most famous work is probably his **Letters and Papers from Prison**, which is concerned with the need for the Christian Church to teach about God in a more secular way, so as to meet the needs of secular society.

Book of Life (NT/C/J): kind of heavenly register, in which God would keep the names of the righteous and remove those of the non-righteous.

The Hebrews believed that God kept such a book (Ps. 69:28). In the New

b

Testament, the phrase occurs six times, and Paul talks of a book which records the names of believers (Phil. 4:3). On *Judgement Day* the dead will be judged and the righteous will have their names entered in the Book of Life (Rev. 20:15).

Brahma/Brahman (H): two closely related terms, both referring to an important aspect of God in Hinduism. (See also *Brahman* entry, below.)

▓ 'Brahman' is a neutral gender and refers to the abstract, impersonal Absolute that is beyond quality ('nirguna') and is the cause of the universe. 'Brahma' is the masculine gender and is, again, the Absolute, but seen as a personal being rather than an abstract power. He is depicted as the first member of the Triad, who creates the universe. He is an important figure in the *Mahabharata*, and in art he is often depicted with four heads, looking in the four directions, and usually holds the prayer-beads and water pot of a priest or the palm-leaf texts of the Veda. In Buddhist cosmology, the idea of a creator god is not accepted and 'Brahma' becomes the title given to the whole range of higher gods.

Brahman (or Brahmin) **(H):** title given to men of the highest of the four Hindu social classes, whose traditional tasks have been to teach and pass on the sacred religious traditions and to perform priestly sacrificial rituals.

▓ For centuries the Brahmans dominated Hindu society, but their position has been threatened in recent years by the lower-*caste* anti-Brahman movements. In English, the term 'Brahman' is sometimes written 'Brahmin'.

▓ *TIP* The wording is very confusing; don't get muddled between 'Brahman' (Absolute) and 'Brahman' (Priest). Many examiners now use the spelling 'Brahmins' to avoid confusion.

breaking of bread (NT/C): important part of the *Eucharist* service which re-enacts Jesus' action in the Last Supper.

▓ In the Last Supper, Jesus took bread, broke it, and gave it to his disciples, saying 'This is my body, given for you; do this in remembrance of me' (Lk 22:19). In the early Church, Christians would share meals together in which they 'broke bread' to display their awareness of the presence of Christ and their remembrance of him (Acts 2:46; 1 Cor. 11:17–34).

Breda, Declaration of (C): declaration made by Charles II at Breda in Holland in 1660.

▓ It promised 'liberty to tender consciences' in those matters of religion which did not actually affect the peace of the realm.

Brethren of the Common Life (C): group formed by Geert de Groote in the fourteenth century to promote a higher level of Christian life and devotion.

▓ The members carried on with their everyday vocations, but also founded many excellent schools offering free education. The most famous members were Jan Busch, Thomas à Kempis and Gabriel Biel.

Buddha (B): Buddhist title meaning, literally, 'one who has woken up', but more commonly translated as 'the enlightened one'.

▓ It is the title most usually given to Siddartha *Gotama*, the historical founder of Buddhism. In fact, according to Buddhist tradition, Gotama is only one in a long line of Buddhas who have appeared, periodically, teaching the same eternal truths. Buddhas are accepted as the highest beings, and the attainment of buddhahood is the culmination of many lifetimes spent as a *Bodhisattva*, perfecting the qualities of patience, wisdom and loving kindness.

Buddhism (B): religious and philosophical movement founded by the Buddha (*Gotama*), who lived in the fifth century BCE in India.

The basic assumptions of Buddhism are the law of *karma* and the liberation from the cycle of rebirth. It seeks to address the problem of universal suffering (*Four Noble Truths*) and offers a system of moral, meditative and mental training aimed at producing a transcendent knowledge which frees the person from selfish concerns. Buddhism does not involve belief in one *omnipotent*, personal God, and it is therefore non-theistic. Today, there are three main Buddhist traditions: the *Theravada* tradition, which is largely found in Sri Lanka and southeast Asia; the 'eastern' tradition, based on *Mahayana* and found in China, Korea and Japan; and the 'northern' tradition, found in Tibet and Mongolia.

Bultmann, Rudolf (1884–1976) (C): German New Testament scholar, regarded by many as the foremost New Testament scholar of modern times, and leading exponent of *form criticism*.

He argued that theologians should be able to interpret the Gospels in the light of modern thought, and suggested that the 'supernatural' elements in the Bible were no longer credible as they stood and should be reinterpreted in the light of modern ideas. He argued, controversially, for the *demythologisation* of the Bible — that is, taking away the element of myth.

burial (OT/J): in biblical times, the custom of disposing of dead bodies quickly due to the heat.

In the Hebrew tradition, the body was washed, anointed, wrapped in a linen cloth and carried in a procession to a grave or tomb. For the poorer people, graves were dug, but caves were also used. The wealthy sometimes arranged for their tombs to be cut out of the rock in a quiet garden location, and the tomb would be sealed with a large stone. Jesus was buried in such a way, in a tomb belonging to Joseph of Arimathea (Matt. 27:57–61). Cremation was not practised by the Hebrews.

burnt offering (OT): special sacrifice to God.

An animal, always male, was killed, and then the whole body was burnt on an altar — only the hide was spared for the priests. It was believed that God would enjoy the smell (Lev. 1:9) of the offering and would, in return, bestow favours upon those making the sacrifice.

calendar (I/J): system for determining the beginning, length, order and divisions of the year.

■ The Islamic calendar is based on lunar months, and the year consists of 354 days. The Muslim era begins from the migration ('hijra') of the prophet Muhammad from Mecca to Medina, which began in September 622 CE, although the year actually begins from the opening of the lunar year in which the migration took place, i.e. 16 July 622 CE.

The Jewish calendar consists of a year made up of 12 lunar months, each of 29 or 30 days. The average year is therefore 354 days long. However, in order for the Jewish festivals, which are based upon the agricultural year, to fall at their appointed times, the lunar year has been brought into line with the solar year by the addition of an extra lunar month in February–March seven times every 19 years.

caliph/caliphate (I): Islamic term for 'successor'.

■ After the death of Muhammad in 632 CE, the caliphs were chosen to lead the Islamic community. Known collectively as the 'caliphate', the caliphs continued for centuries through various lines — the 'Rightly Guided' or 'Orthodox' (632–661 CE), the Umayyad (661–750 CE), and the Abbasid (750–1517 CE). The Ottoman Turkish sultans then took the title for themselves, and it was finally abolished in 1924.

Calvin, John (1509–64) (C): French reformer and theologian, who broke with the Catholic Church after he received a religious experience in which he believed he had received a command to restore the Church to its original purity.

■ His writings, such as ***Institutes of the Christian Religion*** (1536), spoke about the need for a profession of faith from all believers, about regulations concerning admission to the *Lord's Supper*, and advocated the use of excommunication. He emphasised the ultimate importance of faith in God and said that purely intellectual understanding of the scriptures was insufficient for salvation. He believed in the supremacy of religious authority, and in Geneva he sought to establish a regime of religious authority along Old Testament lines. He did this through a series of 'ordinances' which gave power to pastors, elders and deacons, assisted by an ecclesiastical court acting as a tribunal of morals which had the power of excommunication.

Calvinism (C): theological system evolved by *Calvin* which is the basis of most non-Lutheran reformed Churches.

■ It upholds the belief that the Bible is the only rule of faith and that salvation is by faith alone. Religious authority is seen to be superior to state authority.

canon (Greek term meaning a 'rule' or 'standard') **(OT/NT/C):** those books in the Bible which have been recognised as authoritative.

■ This has been an area of great controversy, particularly concerning the acceptance or otherwise of the books of the *Apocrypha*, which were incorporated into the *Vulgate* and retained their authority in the doctrine of the Catholic Church. They were excluded by the Protestant Church during the *Reformation*, when Article 6 of the Anglican Thirty-Nine Articles declared that the Old Testament and the New Testament contained all that was necessary for salvation.

cantor (J): prayer leader of the *synagogue*, particularly on the *Sabbath* and during festivals.

■ He is not a priest, and a layman can carry out this role. In modern times, the increased use of choirs and liturgical music has meant that many cantors are now full-time paid synagogue officials.

caste (H): social status within Hindu society.

■ It is not a religious concept, but is closely related to Hinduism. A person's caste is determined at birth — you are born into either high or low caste — and it brings about certain restrictions. In particular, there are limits on intermarriage between members of different castes. The religious character of caste stems from the theory of *karma*, which is the law of moral cause and effect, and explains why some people are born into high caste and others into low. The highest caste are the *Brahmans*, from which the priesthood comes. Their position at the peak is sanctioned by the sacred texts of the *Vedas*.

■ *TIP* This is a very important concept in Hinduism. However, it is no longer as strictly adhered to as it was in past centuries. Bear this in mind when answering questions on modern Hinduism.

casuistry (OT/E): resolving particular moral dilemmas, especially those involving a conflict of moral rules, by referring to particular cases where the rules apply.

■ In Old Testament times, many laws were framed in a casuistic way. They usually began with an expression like 'If a man...', and went on to outline an offence and give a verdict on it. An example of a casuistic law in the Old Testament would be Lev. 20:9 — 'If a man curses his father or mother, he must be put to death'. In ethics, casuistry is a way of resolving difficult moral issues, or sorting out issues where there is a clash between moral or religious duties. This is usually done by applying general moral principles to particular moral issues.

categorical imperative (E): term introduced by *Kant* concerning the guidance to actions which is given by morality.

Kant spoke of the difference between, on the one hand, carrying out an action in order to achieve a given end (e.g. 'Do X, and Y will be the result'), which he called a 'hypothetical imperative', and, on the other hand, carrying out an action for moral reasons, which he called a 'categorical imperative'. If something is categorical, then it is without condition — so, categorical imperatives are things that should be done without conditions attached — they should not be done to achieve a particular end, but should be done from a sense of morality or duty. For example, the commandment 'You shall not kill' is a categorical imperative, because it requires a person not to kill, even if they want to. Kant's views may be summarised as follows:

(1) Act only on principles which are universal — you should only do something if you are prepared for everyone else to be able to do it as well.

(2) Act in such a way that you treat people as ends and never as means.

categorical statement (E): in ethics, a statement that says what ought to be done in given circumstances, such as 'Do not hunt animals for pleasure, but only for food'.

Catholic (from the Greek for 'general' or 'universal') **(C):** used in one of four different ways within Christianity: (1) to describe the universal church, rather than individual local ones; (2) to describe *orthodox* as opposed to heretical Christians; (3) as a term preferred by Roman Catholics to describe themselves; (4) as a term in contrast to Protestantism, for Churches such as the Roman Catholic Church. It is commonly applied to non-Protestant Churches, such as the Roman Catholic Church, which claim to have a tradition of faith and practice, as opposed to Protestants, who find their ultimate standards in the Bible as interpreted in the principles of the *Reformation*.

Catholic Church (C): largest Church in Western Christianity.

It is made up of a hierarchy of priests and bishops, with the Pope at the head. It places an emphasis on the seven *sacraments* and the *Mass*.

Catholics believe that the first Bishop of Rome was St Peter, on whom, Jesus said, the Church would be built (Matt. 16:18).

Catholics believe in heaven and hell, hold the Virgin Mary and the saints in high esteem, and believe that the bread and wine of the *eucharist* service become the flesh and blood of Christ, through a mystic process called *transubstantiation*.

celibacy (NT/C): state of being unmarried and abstaining from sexual relationships as part of one's devotion to God.

In the New Testament, Paul advocates celibacy as the way to avoid personal troubles, in view of the judgement of the world which he thought was coming (1 Cor. 7).

chagim (J): Jewish term meaning 'festivals'.

The Jewish ritual year begins with the festival of *Rosh Hashanah*, which is a time of repentance and a return to God. Two weeks later (mid-October) is the festival of *Tabernacles*, which remembers the Israelites in the wilderness. This is followed by the annual reading of the *Pentateuch* and 'The Rejoicing of the *Torah*'. Two months later is the festival of Chanukah, which commemorates the revolt of the Maccabees, and this is followed 10 weeks later by Purim, which remembers the deliverance of the Jews as recorded in the Book of Esther. At the beginning of spring, the celebration of Pesach (*Passover*) commemorates the *Exodus*, and 7 weeks later comes Shavuot (*Pentecost*), which marks the revelation of God to Moses at Mount Sinai.

charisma/charismatic (C): gift of grace or of the spirit in Christianity; having that gift.

■ A charismatic church is one in which such spiritual gifts are used in worship and teaching. Members are encouraged to seek these gifts themselves from God and to encourage others. The biblical basis for such belief comes from Paul's teaching in 1 Corinthians 12:1–11.

Chasidism (or Hasidism) **(J):** movement in Judaism which began in the late eighteenth century under the guidance of Israel Baal Shem Tov (the 'Besht') and flourished in eastern Europe.

■ Chasidic teachings were based on a popularised form of the *Kabbalah*, and highlighted the importance of inner service to God through the heart, rather than the strict keeping of Jewish ritual laws. God can be served in everyday activities, and the most important aspect of this service is known as 'devekut', or a cleaving to God in joy. The simple, clear message of Chasidism became popular with ordinary Jews, who could not always understand or aspire to the higher aspects of Jewish lore, but the movement was strongly opposed by rabbinical conservatives, who accused it of *heresy*. Today, Chasidic Jews organise their communities around a Chasidic leader, or 'tzaddik'.

chosen (OT/NT): in the Bible there are many examples of persons or groups who are selected or 'chosen' by God for a particular purpose.

■ In the Old Testament, chosen people include Abraham, Moses and David, and chosen groups include the priests and the people of Israel as a whole, who are the 'chosen people' or the 'people of the *covenant*' (Deut. 7:6).

In the New Testament, the term 'chosen' usually refers to the members of the new Messianic community (Eph. 1:11).

Christ (from the Greek *Christos*, meaning 'anointed one' — a Greek translation of the Hebrew word *Messiah*) **(OT/NT/C):** term which, in Old Testament times, was applied to the king, who was anointed (1 Sam. 16:13).

■ It is a title, not a name, and it was applied to Jesus in the New Testament, as he was seen as being the anointed one who would fulfil the expectations of the Old Testament.

■ *TIP* Remember, 'Christ' is a title — it was **not** Jesus' actual name!

Christian (NT/C): name given to the followers of Christ.

■ It was first used in Antioch around 40 CE, originally by outsiders, to describe Christ's followers (Acts 11:26). The term was certainly used by the people of Rome at the time of the persecutions of Nero in 64 CE, and it became the official

Roman term for describing members of the early Church. Later it was adapted by the Church to distinguish itself from other religions.

Christianity (C): probably the largest world religion, with over 1,000 million members, the biggest single group being the Roman Catholic Church.

◼ Christianity is based upon the life and teaching of Jesus Christ and, through his death, the salvation of humanity. It came out of Judaism, and spread with the work of Paul into the *Gentile* nations. Central to Christianity is the view that God, as a *Trinity*, created the world and saved humanity through the work and sacrifice of his divine son, Jesus. Christianity is a religion with a strong social and moral emphasis, and it seeks to assure believers of life after death and forgiveness of sins.

Christian Socialism (C): nineteenth-century social reform movement initiated by members of the Church of England.

◼ The early Christian Socialists sought to reform both individuals and society as a whole by applying Christian principles in all social reforms. They organised evening classes, developed a 'Working Man's College' in 1854 and opened a cooperative workshop in 1850. The movement was ultimately a failure, however, due to a lack of response from the workers themselves.

Christology (C): study of the person of Christ and, in particular, the question of his divine and human natures.

◼ It has been an area of great controversy, as Christians traditionally believe that Christ is both human and divine, and this has raised questions such as how Jesus can combine both divine and human natures into one unified personality. The best-known Christological declarations have been the Council of Nicea in 325 CE, which defined Jesus as 'of one substance with the Father', and the Council of Chalcedon in 451 CE, which declared that Jesus was 'truly God and truly man...of one substance with the Father as regards his Godhead and...of one substance as regards his manhood'. This definition has been widely criticised, yet not replaced.

Church (C): (1) the universal world-wide community of Christians (Acts 20:28; 1 Cor. 16:1); (2) a local group of Christians in a community.

◼ The New Testament as a whole teaches that the Church was established by Christ as the 'New Israel' (Gal. 6:15) and blessed with the Holy Spirit at *Pentecost*. With the *Reformation* came the notion that the Church is the body, with Christ as the head, whilst at the same time the true Church is an invisible body of those who are saved. In modern times, both among Catholics and Protestants, there has been increased recognition of the need for the organisation of the Church to correspond with the invisible Church, and for the Church to be more detached from the secularisation of the world.

circumcision (*berit milah* in Hebrew) (OT/NTJ): in Judaism, the rite which usually takes place on the eighth day after birth and involves the removal of the foreskin of the penis (Lev. 12:3).

◼ Circumcision represents the sign of the *covenant* between God and the seed of Abraham (Gen. 17:11). In the New Testament, circumcision became a major issue between the early Church and Jewish Christians, who demanded that *Gentile* followers of Christ should first be circumcised. Peter argued against this and his argument prevailed (Acts 15:1–21). It led to the view that the early Church had taken over the role of the 'New Israel' and was not simply a reformed Jewish sect.

Clarendon, Constitutions of (C): sixteen-part enactments put forward by King Henry II to regulate the relations between the Church and secular authorities.

■ They were presented to the Council of Clarendon in 1164, but the Archbishop of Canterbury, Thomas Becket, refused to fix his seal to them. A long dispute followed.

cognitivism (E): term used to specify the notion that there can, in certain areas, be facts that can, in principle, be known.

■ In ethics, it is the view that there are knowable ethical facts. Some writers prefer to use the term 'realism' and use 'cognitivism' only when referring to moral or ethical statements.

commandments (OT/NT): word used in the Bible to refer to the requirements asked for by God and which the people of Israel must keep and obey as a response to God's love (Ps. 119:6–7).

■ The most famous are the *Ten Commandments* (Exod. 20:2–17).

In the New Testament, Jesus stated that the most important of the Ten Commandments were to 'Love the Lord your God ... and Love your neighbour as yourself' (Mk 12:30–31).

The Greek term *Decalogue* is sometimes used to refer to the Ten Commandments.

The word 'commandments' is also used to refer to the people's obligations to their king (2 Kgs 18:18) and children's obligations to parents (Jer. 35:6).

Common Prayer, Book of (C): official service book of the Church of England, containing the daily offices of Morning and Evening Prayer, together with other administrations and rites.

■ The book was compiled because of the need to simplify the Latin service books of the medieval Church and to produce an authoritative book in English. The first such book was issued in 1549 and underwent several changes. The most famous version was produced in 1662 and remained largely unchanged until fairly recent times.

communion (C): in Christianity, term associated with the *Eucharist*, and with the 'coming together' or fellowship within the faith.

■ Specifically, 'communion' is used in the following senses: (1) Holy Communion — an alternative name for the Eucharist; (2) the act of receiving the consecrated bread and wine; (3) the 'Communion of Saints', a fellowship of all Christians in heaven and on earth; (4) a group of specific churches, e.g. the communion of Anglican Churches; and (5) being 'in communion with a church', indicating that each party recognises the other and accepts the sacraments and ministry of the other church.

confession (C): term used in the Christian Church to mean either a profession of faith (Mk 8:29) or, more commonly, an acknowledgement of sin.

▨ Confession may be done in a general way by a congregation in a liturgical service, or by an individual in private — for example, making a confession to a priest. The formal act of forgiveness offered by a priest is known as 'absolution'.

Congregationalism (C): form of church government by which each local church is seen to be autonomous and independent.

▨ Congregationalism dates from the *Reformation* and grew despite periodic persecution. Today, Congregational Churches do not act in complete isolation. In 1972 the majority of such Churches in England and Wales united with the Presbyterian Church to form the United Reformed Church.

conscience (E): said to be the way in which people judge their own moral actions — in a sense, a method of choosing right from wrong.

▨ It is a subjective method; that is, it only works for the individual — you cannot use your conscience to judge the actions of others, only yourself. Conscience may be given a religious dimension by suggesting that, in some way, it is a link with God — a 'small voice' within us.

consecration (C): in Christianity, the act of separating people or things from profane use and dedicating them to the service of God (Exod. 29).

▨ In modern times, this is seen in several ways: (1) at the *Eucharist*, the act whereby the bread and wine become the body and blood of Christ; (2) when a Bishop takes his office; (3) when a church or altar is set apart exclusively for the service of God.

consequentialism (E): ethical theory concerned with determining right from wrong, using the consequences of an action as a guide.

▨ It appears in two main forms: (1) a person is responsible for their actions and for unintended but foreseeable consequences — for instance, if you shoot at a particular person in a crowded room and hit someone else by mistake, you are still responsible, since hitting another person was foreseeable in that circumstance; (2) an action is right if, and only if, its total outcome is the best possible outcome. Thus, the essential point is that it is the consequences alone which should be taken into account when making judgements about what is right and wrong.

▨ *TIP* This word is used a lot in *utilitarianism* questions, and sometimes words such as 'right' and 'wrong' are replaced by words such as 'duty' and 'obligation'.

contingent (P): in philosophy, the term used to describe a fact or event which depends (is contingent) upon another fact or event happening first.

▨ For instance, humans are 'contingent' beings since they depend on other things, e.g. air and food, in order to exist.

conversion (NT/C): change to another religion, which often involves a change of lifestyle.

▨ In the New Testament there are many examples of conversions, the most famous being Paul's conversion on the road to Damascus (Acts 9:1–19). Such conversions would normally be followed by baptism. Throughout the history of Christianity there have been examples of both dramatic and gentle conversion experiences, often as a result of deep prayer and meditation.

Corinth/Corinthian (NT): capital of the Roman province of Achaia (now in modern Greece); someone from Corinth.

■ Corinth was a very important commercial centre. Paul established a Christian Church there in about 50 CE and it included many Jewish converts and Greek-speaking *Gentiles*. The New Testament contains two letters ('epistles') sent by Paul to this early Church. In the first, called 1 Corinthians, Paul deals with a variety of issues which were causing problems, including worship, spiritual gifts, sexual relationships, love and marriage, the *Eucharist* and the *resurrection* of the dead. In the second, called 2 Corinthians, he looks at his own status as an Apostle, and at the issue of morality in the Church.

Corporation Act 1661 (C): Act requiring members of municipal corporations to declare the 'Solemn League and Covenant' to be null and unlawful and to affirm that they had received *Communion* according to the rites of the Church of England in the year preceding their election.

■ The Act was part of a reaction against the 'Solemn League and Covenant', which was an agreement made in 1643 between the Scottish and English Parliaments concerning the status of the Church.

cosmological argument (P): argument that attempts to prove the existence of God by suggesting that everything has a cause, which in turn has a cause, and assumes that there must be a 'first cause' which does not itself have a cause — that is God.

■ The argument takes as its starting point the fact that there is a universe, and goes on to explain why there should be anything at all. The most famous expositions of the cosmological argument are those of St Thomas *Aquinas* in his 'Five Ways', which he described in his work **Summa Theologica**.

■ *TIP* This is a crucial argument in philosophy of religion examinations and is often asked in contrast with the *teleological* and *ontological arguments*. You must ensure that you know not only the views of Aquinas, Leibnitz and *Kant*, but also the strengths and weaknesses of the argument as a whole. Also, make sure you can spell it properly — it is the most common misspelling in the examination!

counsellor (NT): term sometimes used in the New Testament to refer to the *Holy Spirit*. It highlights the Spirit's work as a help to believers in times of trial (Jn 14:16).

■ *TIP* Sometimes the term 'advocate' is used, from the Greek *paraclete/paracletos*, meaning one who will stand beside the defendant in a court of law.

Counter-Reformation (C): sixteenth-century movement of reform and revival within the Roman Catholic Church in Europe and an attack against the *Reformation*.

■ The first signs were the appearance of new religious orders in the 1520s, such as the Capuchins and the Barnabites, one of the most energetic being the Jesuit order, which became a great missionary force within Europe, Asia and the Americas. The Council of Trent (1562–63) redefined doctrine and marked the triumph of the papacy over opposition groups. *Heresy* was repressed by special tribunals such as the Spanish Inquisition. Perhaps the greatest triumph of the Counter-Reformation was the return to the Roman Catholic Church of southern Germany and Poland. The movement lasted until the middle of the seventeenth century.

covenant (OT/NT): agreement entered into voluntarily by two parties in which each pledges to do something for the other, with certain conditions usually imposed.

It is a very important notion in the Old Testament, which is largely the story of the covenant between God and the people of Israel. God made a covenant with Noah (Gen. 9:8–17) and later with Abraham (Gen. 17:1–27), which was sealed by circumcision. In both cases, the Old Testament stresses the element of *grace* on the part of God — no rigorous conditions were imposed upon the people. However, it was the covenant made at Mount Sinai that highlighted the responsibilities of the agreement (Exod. 19:5). This was a 'conditional' type of agreement — God would be the God of Israel and the people who obey his Law. The agreement was kept in the Ark of the Covenant. The details can be found in Exodus 21–24. The Old Testament tells of how the people of Israel often break their side of the agreement and the *prophets* continually call to the people to remember their covenant obligations. There was also a 'promise' type of covenant between God and King David (the 'Davidic Covenant') assuring the king of the permanence of his dynasty if the Law was obeyed (1 Kgs 2:2–4). A new covenant is established by Jesus in the New Testament (Mk 14:24; 1 Cor. 11:25), based on his atoning sacrifice.

Cranmer, Thomas (1489–1556) (C): Archbishop of Canterbury under Henry VIII.

He annulled Henry's marriages to Catherine of Aragon and Anne Boleyn, and later officiated over Henry's marriage and divorce from Anne of Cleves. After Henry's death, he became an important counsellor of Edward VI and was largely responsible for the ***Book of Common Prayer*** (1549), the abolition of old Church ceremonies and the destruction of images. He was instrumental in the writing of the ***Forty-Two Articles*** (1553), which were a collection of Anglican doctrinal formulas. He was tried for *heresy* in the reign of Mary and was burnt at the stake in 1556.

Creed (C): very precise and formal statement of important points of doctrine and belief.

In Christianity, summaries of Christian belief can be found in the New Testament (1 Cor. 15:3–6; 1 Tim. 3:16). They are contained in two forms within the Church, the Apostle's Creed and the Nicene Creed, which were formulated in the centuries following the establishment of the Christian Church as expressions of belief for new members and candidates for *baptism*, and as a method of excluding heretical views.

The Apostle's Creed is a statement of faith used in the Western Church; it has three sections dealing with God the Father, Jesus Christ and the Holy Spirit. The **Book of Common Prayer** orders its use at the services of Matins and Evensong.

The Nicene Creed was issued in 325 CE by the Council of Nicaea and was drawn up to defend the orthodox Christian faith against movements such as Arianism. It is often used in the *Eucharist* service.

cross (C): symbol of the Christian faith.

Jesus was crucified on a cross of wood, and the Cross has become a symbol to Christians of God's love and the defeat of evil, and a reminder of the need for Christians to follow the example of Jesus.

crucifixion (NT/C): method of execution used by the Romans that involved nailing or binding a victim to a cross made of wood and then leaving them to die.

Jesus Christ suffered death in this way (Lk 23:26–49). In Christian theology, the Crucifixion is very important — the death of Jesus is seen as a sacrifice to deal with sin, and Christians, by *baptism*, share in what Christ experienced on the Cross and undergo their own 'death'; to sin and begin a new life (1 Cor. 1:23; Gal. 3:13). The signs of the cross or crucifix in Christianity symbolise the sacrificial death of Christ.

crusades (C): series of European military expeditions during medieval times against non-Christians and heretics, sanctioned by the Pope.

The main crusades were those undertaken by European rulers, 1096–1291, in Palestine to recover the Christian holy places, such as Jerusalem, from the forces of Islam. Subsequent crusades were attempts to gain land and improve commerce, or were used to attack heretics and non-Christians in Europe. The Knights Templar, founded in 1118, was a military order which arose from the crusades.

curtains (OT/NT): used in biblical times to separate people from the presence of God.

In the Old Testament, the *tabernacle*, or dwelling place of God, was a portable sanctuary formed by ten curtains, decorated with figures of angels (Exod. 26:1–36).

In the New Testament, Herod's *Temple* in Jerusalem contained the 'Holy of Holies', the most sacred place, which was divided from the rest of the Temple by a curtain, which acted as a symbolic 'barrier' to keep people away from the presence of God. At the moment of Jesus' death, it is said that this curtain was ripped in two, showing that his death had removed the barrier between God and humanity (Lk 23:45).

Dana (B): Buddhist term meaning 'giving', seen as a powerful remedy to attachment and selfishness.

▓ It usually refers to giving that is directed towards the 'three jewels' of Buddhism (Buddha, *dhamma* and *Sangha*), and is an important feature of Buddhist practice amongst laypeople. It is usually done through the giving of robes, food, medicines and lodgings to members of the Sangha.

darshana (H): Hindu term meaning 'seeing' (as in 'insight') — one of the six salvation-philosophies of Hinduism.

▓ In particular, darshana is the recognition of the nature of things and the overcoming of illusion, which will set the believer on the path of salvation.

Darwinism (P): name sometimes given to the theories of Charles Darwin (1809–82).

▓ Darwin's main theories are found in his works ***On the Origin of Species by Means of Natural Selection*** (1859) and ***The Descent of Man*** (1871). His views on evolution caused great debate and controversy, since they cast doubts on the biblical accounts of the Creation and seemed to disprove the idea that God created the world.

Dasam Granth (also called the 'Book of the Tenth Guru') **(S):** substantial collection of work, second to the *Adi Granth* in Sikh scripture, probably written by Guru Gobind Singh.

▓ It includes the retelling of the *Krishna* legends.

David (d. c. 970 BCE) (OT/NT): remembered in the Old Testament as Israel's ideal king and in the New Testament as the ancestor of Christ (Matt. 1:17; Rom. 1:3).

▓ He was the shepherd son of Jesse and came to fame when he apparently killed the *Philistine* champion, Goliath (1 Sam. 17:1–51). He served as a musician in King Saul's court, married the King's daughter and became friends with the King's son, Jonathan. He was anointed by Samuel for the future kingship. After Saul's death at the age of 30 he became king and later captured the city of Jerusalem and made it his capital, restoring the *Ark* of the Covenant and providing a central sanctuary for corporate worship. His reign of 33 years was something of a 'Golden Age', and he extended the country's borders, ended the Philistine threat and increased prosperity. His illicit relationship with

d

Bathsheba led to the birth of their son, Solomon. David's story is contained in 1 Samuel 16–1 Kings 2.

In the New Testament, Jesus is referred to as the 'Son of David', in the light of the Jewish belief that the Messiah would be descended from David.

■ *TIP* A very important figure, but remember that David's story is an idealised one in the Bible and there are many contradictions (e.g. the slaying of Goliath). Be careful before accepting the accounts on their face value. Questions may contrast David's early successes with later problems and the issue of his private life (e.g. Bathsheba).

day of the Lord (OT/NT): in the Old Testament, the popular belief that a day would come when God would intervene in human history and free Israel from fear and oppression.

■ The eighth-century prophet Amos, however, said that the people were exploiting the poor and following false ideas, and warned that the day of the Lord would be one of judgement (Amos 5:18). After that judgement, there would be a time when God's rule would be established all over the earth.

In the New Testament, Paul uses the term 'day of the Lord Jesus' (Rom. 2:5) to describe the judgement which lies ahead.

deacon (from the Greek *diakonos*, meaning 'servant') **(NT):** position in the Christian Church ranking just below a priest.

■ The first 'Seven Deacons' were appointed in Acts 6 by the early Church to assist the Apostles and serve the poor. Later, their functions were increased to include administrative and liturgical functions. In the Western Church today, 'deacon' is a title usually given to someone preparing for the priesthood. In the Lutheran Church, deacons are assistant ministers.

Dead Sea Scrolls (C): name given to the remains of a large collection of Hebrew and Aramaic manuscripts which were discovered in caves at Qumran, near the Dead Sea, in 1947.

■ They contain much of the Old Testament, together with other works not previously known, including a series of commentaries, 'Psalms of Thanksgiving', an apocalyptic work called 'The War of the Sons of Light against the Sons of Darkness', a 'Manual of Discipline' and the 'Damascus Fragments'. The scrolls belonged to the Jewish community, probably of *Essenes*, who lived at Qumran at the time of Jesus, and are dated at between 20 BCE and 70 CE. They are of considerable importance in assisting our understanding of the Bible and of life in those times.

Decalogue (OT): Greek word for the *Ten Commandments*, which are the laws given to Moses by God on two stone tablets (Exod. 24:12 and 34:4) and kept in the *Ark* of the Covenant.

■ Considerable detail was added to the laws over the years, but the Decalogue remained in an easy-to-remember form for the people. The commandments require the people to worship only the God of Israel, and contain rules of social and religious behaviour.

Decapolis (NT): name given to the territory of ten Greek cities which were located east of the Sea of Galilee.

■ It was a cosmopolitan area of many languages and cultures. Jesus is recorded as having passed through it in Mark 7:31.

de dicto (P): philosophical term meaning 'concerning the word/expression'.

■ It is usually applied in reference to the *ontological argument* for the existence of God, which asks whether God is 'de dicto' necessary — in other words, does the word 'God' render his existence necessary. For instance, if we say that the attributes of God include his eternity, or immortality, then in a real sense he must exist, otherwise he could not be eternal or immortal. 'De dicto' contrasts with the term '*de re*'.

deism (P): belief in God as a perfect, personal being.

■ The originator of deism in England was Herbert of Cherbury who wrote in the 1620s of five basic notions: (1) there is one supreme God; (2) God ought to be worshipped; (3) worship consists in virtue and piety; (4) sins should be repented; (5) God rewards and punishes. In the seventeenth century, many deists were accused by the Church of rejecting belief in revelation, miracles, providence and immortality. In fact, many deists disagreed with each other — their common bond seemed to have been that they accepted only those religious beliefs which they considered to be rational. More recently, deism has come to mean a belief that God created the world at the beginning but does not intervene in the course of natural and human affairs.

■ *TIP* In examination questions, deism may be contrasted with such notions as *atheism* and *polytheism*.

democracy (from the Greek *demokratia*, meaning 'rule by the people') **(E):** system of government in which all citizens are entitled to participate in political decision-making, usually through elected representatives.

demythologisation (NT): term used by Rudolf *Bultmann* (1884–1976) to explain the way in which the 'real' truth of the New Testament could be acceptable to modern readers.

■ Bultmann's view was that the New Testament was written by authors who had a different view of the world and a different cultural background, and that people today have different views and backgrounds and therefore the meaning of the New Testament becomes questionable. He sought to 'demythologise' the New Testament — that is, to identify the myths and supernatural events (the Virgin Birth, for instance) because they are not historical facts, but are the means by which the meanings of the authors are disclosed. He argued that the New Testament must be reinterpreted in ways more appropriate for modern readers.

de re (P): philosophical term meaning 'concerning the thing (itself)'.

■ It is most commonly used in the *cosmological argument* for the existence of God, where it is argued that God's necessary existence is based on the 'nature of things'. Thus, if we say that the universe was created and then say that God is the Supreme Creator, then, if the universe exists, God exists too (or at least, God existed at the time of the creation of the universe).

design argument (P): philosophical argument for the existence of God.

■ It has two steps: (1) from our observation of the world around us, we may conclude that there is an order or design in nature; (2) if there is design, then there must be a designer, whom we identify as 'God'.

■ *TIP* A very important concept in philosophy of religion. It is sometimes called the *teleological argument*. In examination questions, it may be contrasted with the *ontological* and *cosmological arguments*. Ensure that you know not only what the design argument is, but also its strengths and weaknesses.

determinism (P): notion that all events are determined by previous existing causes.

Devotio Moderna (Latin for 'modern devotion') **(C):** revival of spiritual life which took place at the end of the fourteenth century in Holland, led by a group calling themselves the 'Brethren of the Common Life'.

■ The emphasis was on the inner life of the believer, and methodical meditation was encouraged. The principal representatives were the 'Windesheim Canons'.

dhamma/dharma (H/B): term used in both Hinduism and Buddhism to mean an understanding of the way things truly are.

■ The Buddha's teachings amount to an understanding of the way things truly are and are referred to as dhamma; they also offer a way to practise dhamma that leads to the seeing of dhamma. Thus to follow the teaching is to practise dhamma and to attain enlightenment is to realise dhamma. For Buddhists, the failure to recognise dhamma means that your world view is wrong and this leads to suffering. Dhamma is one of the 'three refuges' of Buddhism ('*tisarana*').

Dhammapada (meaning 'sayings of *dhamma*') **(B):** one of the three books which belong to the 'Sutta' section of the Buddhist scriptures.

■ It is a book of over 400 verses, which covers many aspects of Buddhist teaching and traditions associated with the Buddha.

dhanb (I): term in Islam meaning 'sin'.

■ The *Qur'an* says that humankind shares in Adam's original sinfulness, and that all sins are disobedience to God and show ingratitude for God's goodness. The supreme sin is called 'shirk' and refers to *polytheism* and denial of God's unity. This sin is unforgivable. The Qur'an talks of grave sins ('kabira'), which may evoke punishment from God, and lesser sins, which do not affect a person's faith.

Diaspora (Greek for 'a scattering') **(NT):** term used to describe the Jewish people who lived outside Palestine in biblical times.

■ The Diaspora began when many Jews were deported to Assyria in the eighth century BCE and later, in the sixth century BCE, to Babylon. Many of these Jews settled down and did not return to Palestine. By the time of Christ, Jews lived all over the Roman Empire (Jn 7:35) and many spoke Greek. These Jews were still loyal to Jerusalem, paying *Temple* taxes and visiting the Temple (Acts 2:5).

disciple (NT): pupil, in the sense of a follower of a teacher.

■ Being a disciple was common in biblical times, and many prophets and teachers had disciples. In the New Testament, John the Baptist had disciples (Mk 2:18), and the word is particularly used to describe those who accompanied Jesus (Mk 6:1). Of these, the most important are the 'Twelve', namely Peter, Andrew, James, John, Philip, Bartholomew, Matthew, Thomas, James (son of Alphaeus), Simon the Zealot, Judas (son of James) and Judas Iscariot (Lk 6:14–16). They not only learned from Jesus, but also had the power to teach and to heal (Lk 9:1).

discourse ethics (E): theory which seeks to establish the right moral and political principles.

■ The right principles are said to be those which arise by means of communication taking place under specified ideal conditions. These conditions are: (1) the parties should regard each other as equals; (2) there must be no force or pressure; (3) the only form of persuasion should be rational argument; (4) all assumptions can be questioned; (5) assumptions are only accepted if both sides agree; (6) communication must be open-ended and nobody has the authority to declare the issue settled for ever. The leading supporters of this approach are Jurgen Habermas and Karl-Otto Apel.

Dissolution of the Monasteries (C): act ordered by Henry VIII (1536) which abolished the monastery system in England in order to replenish Henry's treasury and to facilitate the establishment of royal supremacy.

■ The Act for the Dissolution of the Smaller Monasteries (1536) ordered the suppression of 250 religious establishments, and the Act for the Dissolution of the Greater Monasteries (1539) vested the other monasteries in the Crown.

Divine Right of Kings (C): Christian political doctrine that the hereditary monarch has a divine right to the Crown and that if a subject rebels against them it is a political crime and a sin against God.

■ In England, this right was strongly upheld by the Stuarts in the seventeenth century until the reign of James II (1685–88) after his attack on the Church of England.

docetism (C): view that Jesus was, in fact, a divine being who only appeared to be human.

■ It derived from the Hellenistic notion of *dualism*, which contains the idea that the created world, the 'flesh', is tainted, physical and perishable, whereas the realm of God is good, spiritual and immortal. Since Jesus came from the divine realm, claimed docetists, he could not be truly human. Some scholars claim that John's Gospel contains docetic ideas, particularly in chapter 17. They suggest that Jesus is portrayed within the Gospel as lacking in human characteristics and is never properly exposed to sickness and suffering. He is so heavily portrayed as being on the 'side of God' that he does not seem truly human. Against this, other scholars point out that one of the major characteristics of John's Gospel is the claim that Jesus is 'the Word made flesh' (Jn 1:14) and that Jesus' humanity is seen in references to his earthly family (Jn 2:1 and

7:3), as well as his tiredness (Jn 4:6), his grief (Jn 11:35) and his death. Docetists were branded as heretics by *Ignatius Loyola*.

doctrinal (C): referring to a body of beliefs accepted by the Church.

■ Different Churches and denominations may have different doctrinal beliefs on, for example, the person of Christ.

dualism (P): belief that there are two opposing forces in the universe and in the nature of human beings — for example, light and dark, good and evil, flesh and spirit, mind and body.

dukkha (B): Buddhist term, usually translated as 'suffering'.

■ It implies a sense of 'unease' that, it is felt, spoils apparently pleasant experiences — ultimately, dukkha characterises the suffering caused by the cycle of rebirth. It is, along with *anatta* and *anicca*, one of the three marks of conditioned existence.

Durga (meaning 'Unassailable') **(H):** one of the most important Hindu deities.

■ She is best known as Mahishasuramardini, the slayer of the Buffalo Demon. In art, Durga is shown with many arms, holding weapons but smiling gently on her worshippers.

Easter (C): feast of the *Resurrection* — the earliest and greatest Christian festival, commemorating the death and resurrection of Jesus.

■ The date of Easter is movable and is determined by the Paschal Full Moon. It occurs between 21 March and 25 April.

Good Friday is remembered as the day of crucifixion, and Easter Sunday commemorates the Resurrection.

ecumenical movement (C): movement mainly within Protestantism which has sought to promote understanding and, in some cases, union between Christian Churches.

■ The modern ecumenical movement dates from the Edinburgh Conference of 1910, which led to the establishment of the International Missionary Council and, later, the *World Council of Churches*. It found greatest support among Protestant Churches. However, following the *Second Vatican Council* in 1964, the participation of Roman Catholics has been more forthcoming. Regional and national councils of Churches have been formed in most parts of the world.

Eightfold Path (B): traditionally regarded as the Buddha's first teaching — 'the way leading to the cessation of suffering'.

■ The Eightfold Path comprises right view, right intention, right action, right speech, right livelihood, right effort, right mindfulness and right concentration. These eight items cover the three dimensions of Buddhist practice — wisdom, conduct and concentration — which together are capable of producing an inner transformation of the individual.

■ *TIP* The Eightfold Path represents headings for aspects of Buddhist practice. It describes what a Buddhist seeks to develop rather than how he or she sets about doing it.

election (NT/C): biblical notion that God selects (elects) people to serve his purposes for the world.

■ In the Old Testament, this 'election' includes individuals such as Abraham (Gen. 12) and the Jews themselves as 'the Chosen People'.

In the New Testament, God is seen to choose a single individual, Christ, to fulfil his purposes. When his work is completed, then the number of believers will expand and 'God's chosen people' (presumably the Christian Church) will replace the old with the new (1 Peter 2:9). In other words, the Church becomes the New Israel.

Elohim (Hebrew for 'gods') **(OT):** word used in the Old Testament to refer to the God of Israel.

■ It is used in its plural form to show the majesty of God. It can be found in certain sources of Genesis 22 and Exodus 3. The singular form 'El' is used in the Book of Job.

emotivism (E): sometimes called 'the emotive theory of ethics', the theory that there are no ethical facts and no ethical knowledge.

■ It suggests that ethical statements are neither true nor false and instead simply express emotions, desires or attitudes. The theory was first proposed by Axel Hagerstrom (1868–1939), in his 1911 lecture 'On the truth of moral ideas', and later developed by Alfred *Ayer* and the American philosopher Charles Stevenson (1908–79) in his 1944 work *Ethics and Language*.

empiricism (P): view that all knowledge is based upon, or comes from, experience; it rejects irrationality and superstition.

■ David *Hume* and John Stuart *Mill* are important empiricists.

■ *TIP* The main problem with empiricism is that certain aspects of 'knowledge' that empiricism has to take account of are themselves theoretical and not empirically based, e.g. time and space.

emptiness (B): important Buddhist concept, often used in reference to meditation to highlight its peaceful nature, which is free from noisy distractions and other disturbances.

■ The term is also used to refer to an insight into the emptiness of phenomena and to the transcendent mind, which is empty of greed and delusion.

enlightenment (P): (1) to become aware, by knowledge or by religion; (2) the Enlightenment — a period in eighteenth-century philosophical thinking, where belief in human reason and progress was encouraged and older values of tradition and authority were questioned.

■ An example of enlightenment is the Buddha, the 'Enlightened One'.

epistemic distance (P): concept that God has created humanity at a distance, to keep us away from knowledge of him.

■ The theory suggests that God has placed this distance between humanity and himself in order that we can choose to come to him, rather than be overwhelmed with evidence of him, which would leave us no choice but to believe.

Erasmus, Desiderius (1469–1536) (C): humanist and one of the foremost scholars of his age.

■ He is remembered for his writings against Martin *Luther* on free will, during the *Reformation*. He also wrote *Praise of Folly* (1509), which was a satire on *monasticism* and the corruption of the Church, and in 1516 he produced a Greek New Testament. Erasmus is seen by many as having paved the way for the Reformation through his satires.

eschatology (from the Greek *ta eschata*, meaning 'the doctrine of the last things') **(OT/NT):** term used in reference to Christian discourses which deal with death, judgement, the individual soul and the fate of humanity in general.

In the Old Testament, the main references to eschatology come in the so-called 'apocalyptic' writings, such as the Book of Daniel, and in the writings of the prophets which talk about the 'day of the Lord', judgement, national repentance, the punishment of the wicked and future hope.

In the New Testament, eschatology covers many of the complex ideas concerning the *kingdom of God*, the coming of the *Son of Man*, divine judgement and the age to come.

Essenes (NT): group within Judaism that originated in the second century BCE and lasted until after the Jewish Wars in 70 CE.

They are mentioned by the Jewish historian Josephus (37–100 CE). They were a very religious group, who were controlled by a priestly leadership and observed the law strictly. Some Essenes lived in villages, and most scholars believe that the *Qumran* community was made up of Essenes. The Essenes believed themselves to be 'sons of light' and were waiting to fight for the forces of God in the Final Battle.

eternal life (NT/C): term used in Christianity to refer to a personal relationship with God which lasts for ever.

In the New Testament, eternal life is the 'reward' of one's faith and actions in this life (Jn 10:28). Aspects of eternal life may be experienced in this life through the believer's relationship with God, but eternal life can only be fully received after the believer has passed through death (2 Tim. 2:13) into the *Resurrection* on the last day.

TIP The term 'eternal life' is often interchangeable in Christianity with the term 'everlasting life'. The important point to note is that eternal/everlasting life is based on a relationship with God. It is not, therefore, the same as immortality, which is a more philosophical term meaning to live for ever.

ethical egoism (E): ethical theory which provides that a person ought always to act in their own best interests.

An 'egoist' is a person who is exclusively or excessively concerned with their own personal gain or advantage. For egoists, an action is right if, and only if, it benefits the person carrying it out.

ethical relativism (E): (1) the notion that individuals, groups and societies can differ in their view of what is right and wrong or good and bad in relation to character and conduct; (2) the notion that what is regarded as good or bad, right or wrong depends on the situation.

An example of the first definition is that in some societies it is acceptable for a man to have more than one wife, whilst in others it is not.

An example of the second definition is the view that it is wrong to kill in peacetime, but right to do so in wartime.

ethics (from the Greek *ethos*, meaning 'habit' or 'custom') **(E):** philosophical study of the moral value of human conduct and the rules and principles that should govern it.

▨ The term is used in several ways: (1) normative ethics — the view that standards of good and bad, right and wrong should be accepted by a 'class' of individuals — this 'class' might be the whole human race or, in the field of medicine, all doctors; (2) social or religious ethics — the view that there is a body of doctrine concerning good and bad, right and wrong, which all those who claim to belong to a particular 'class' should follow, for instance that Christians should adhere to Christian ethics; (3) meta-ethics — the view that ethical concepts are the objects of philosophical inquiry and that ideas of good and bad, right and wrong should be analysed to discover if ethical truths can really be known.

Eucharist (from the Greek *eukharistos*, meaning 'thankful') **(C):** the central act of Christian worship — a rite of fellowship and *communion*.

▨ It stems from the Last Supper (Mk 14:12–26; Lk 22:7–38), at which Jesus gave thanks, broke bread and gave it to his disciples to eat, saying 'This is my body'. He then gave them wine, telling them to drink it, as 'This is my blood'. The institution of the Eucharist is recorded in 1 Corinthians 11:17–34. During the Eucharist service, the participants eat bread and sip wine as an act of thanksgiving for the whole of God's work in creation and redemption, and to participate in the sacrifice of Christ. The actual significance and importance of the Eucharist has been a subject of considerable controversy through the ages.

▨ *TIP* Other names for the Eucharist are *Mass*, Holy Communion and the *Lord's Supper*.

eugenics (from the Greek *eugenes*, meaning 'well born') **(E):** term first used by Francis Galton in his book **Hereditary Genius** (1869) to refer to the scientific inquiry into the hereditary factors which determine how people are 'made up'.

▨ In modern times, interest has grown considerably. In the early part of the twentieth century it was suggested that if humans were 'selectively bred', i.e. unions made between persons with the finest physical or mental qualities, then 'better' human beings might be produced — an idea which led to much controversy. More recently, the eugenics debate has centred over the possibilities of embryo selection and genetic engineering in order to fight disease and disability.

euthanasia (from the Greek *eu*, meaning good, and *thanatos*, meaning death) **(E):** notion of bringing about a painless death to a person.

▨ It is a very controversial area, for it deals with the possibility of allowing, for example, the very ill or seriously handicapped to die without using medical treatment to prolong their lives. There are two main types: (1) voluntary euthanasia (assisted suicide) — helping a person who wishes to die to do so; (2) involuntary euthanasia — assisting someone to die to 'put them out of their misery', usually when they are unable to request this for themselves. Euthanasia is opposed by moral theologians and many Christians on the grounds that it conflicts with the sixth commandment and is a denial of the Christian attitude towards suffering.

evangelicalism (C): in its widest sense, the term applies to those Protestant Churches which claim to base their teaching primarily on the Gospel; in particular, within the Church of England it is applied to those Christians who lay special importance on personal conversion and salvation by faith in the *atonement* offered by Christ through his crucifixion.

evil (OT/NT/P): generally seen as the 'going wrong' of something which is inherently good — usually involving suffering and, in Christian terms, sometimes attributed to disobedience to God's will or to natural disasters.

▓ According to the Bible, evil began with the disobedience of Adam and Eve in Eden and continues wherever the human race conflicts with the will of God — in the Old Testament, disasters and suffering are sometimes depicted as a punishment from God (Ps. 78:49).

The power of evil is said to be under the control of beings with a leader, sometimes called Satan. These beings are rebels against God and can take over the lives of people through demonic possession (Lk 8:26–39). Evil is also found within the human spirit (Mk 7:20–23) and can appear in human thoughts and actions. At *Judgement Day* there will be the destruction of all that is evil (Rev. 19:11).

In philosophy, the problem of evil revolves around the notion that if God is loving and all-powerful, then he should prevent evil. However, since there is evil in the world, then perhaps God is either not loving or not powerful enough to prevent it. Attempts to resolve this problem and to show that God can be loving and all-powerful, yet still allow for evil, are called 'theodicies'.

▓ *TIP* Most scholars agree that there are two 'types' of evil — physical or natural evil, such as earthquakes and other acts of nature, and moral evil, such as war and murder, which are the acts of human beings.

ex deo (P): philosophical term meaning 'out of God'.

Exile (OT): refers to the Jewish Exile which began in 597 BCE when the Babylonians under King Nebuchadnezzar captured Jerusalem and sent the citizens to Babylon.

▓ In 587 and 582 BCE, after the Jewish authorities failed to heed the advice of the prophet Jeremiah to accept Babylonian rule, uprisings took place which were crushed by the Babylonians, and more Jews were sent into exile. The Exile ended in 538 BCE, when King Cyrus of Persia conquered Babylon and the Jews were allowed to return.

existentialism (P): in its religious form, the chief exponent was Soren Kierkegaard (1813–55), who advocated a very personal approach to religion, with the emphasis on faith, emotion and commitment.

▓ Kierkegaard stressed the importance of a 'leap of faith' by the individual, rather than seeking intellectual and rational truth. He believed that faith was the most important aspect of Christianity, and he attacked theologians who tried to show that Christianity was a rational religion. For Kierkegaard, the most important thing was not intellectual understanding, but the 'subjective truth' of our own existence. Kierkegaard's ideas were taken up by others, such as Karl *Barth*.

ex nihilo (Latin, meaning 'out of nothing') **(P):** usually used to refer to the way in which God apparently created the world 'out of nothing' (Gen. 1:2).

Exodus (OT/J): refers to the departure from Egypt by the Israelites under the leadership of Moses — and the account of this event is largely retold in the Book of Exodus in the Old Testament.

■ The Israelites had lived in Egypt for about 430 years and had been enslaved by the Egyptians. After a series of plagues had struck Egypt, the Pharaoh had reluctantly allowed the Israelites to go free. The historical dating is unclear, but many scholars place the date of the Israelites' departure somewhere in the thirteenth century BCE. The Exodus lasted for 40 years, during which time the Israelites wandered in the desert wilderness and received the Law and the covenant at Mount Sinai. The Exodus ends with the entry into the Promised Land of Canaan. The Exodus is a very important event in Judaism and is seen as the outstanding instance of God's work with his Chosen People. The festivals of *Passover*, *Pentecost* and *Tabernacles* are based on events associated with the Exodus.

exorcism (NT): the removal of evil spirits from a person.

■ At the time of Christ it was believed that evil spirits could take possession of a person and cause them physical or mental illness. By exorcism, the demon could be 'cast out' and the person cured. Jesus is often depicted performing exorcisms (Mk 1:21–28), and he gave his disciples the same power (Matt. 10:1). Following the example of Christ, the Christian Church has continued to perform exorcisms. Such exorcisms do not necessarily mean that a person is possessed by demons, but are, more commonly, special prayers asking for evil to be restrained.

Ezekiel (OT): a prophet who lived at the time of the *Exile*.

■ He was called by God, whilst in exile in Babylon, to give a message of repentance and future hope. He stressed the need for the people to be made new from the heart and offered a vision of holiness in the future, when the people would once again worship in the Temple (Ezek. 40–48).

fact dualism (E): the view that statements of fact are of a different kind from statements of value and that no statement of the second kind can be inferred from the first kind. In other words, even if we have the facts, the evaluation of those facts remains open.

■ For example, if we make the factual statement 'Dogs have four legs' and the value statement 'My dog is friendly', you cannot infer from the first statement that all dogs are 'friendly'.

faith (OT/NT): in its biblical sense, trust in God.

■ In the Old Testament, faith was the basis of the *covenant* — the Israelites would have faith in God and, in turn, their faithfulness would be rewarded. The faith of certain individuals, such as Abraham and David, are highlighted, along with the warnings from the prophets that without faith, the people of Israel would not survive (Is. 30:15).

In the New Testament, faith is defined in Hebrews 11:1 — it is where the believer accepts to be true those realities which are invisible: 'Now faith is being sure of what we hope for and certain of what we do not see.' These 'realities' are belief in God and salvation through Christ who, according to St Paul, is 'the author and perfecter of our faith' (Heb. 12:2). Jesus himself is said to be able to heal the sick, thanks to the faith of themselves or their family (Mk 9:23–24).

Membership of the Christian Church is based on faith.

■ *TIP* A very important concept. Examination questions often use faith as a basis for questions — for example, concerning Abraham as a 'man of faith', or about the teachings of the prophets, such as Amos and Hosea, on the consequences of a lack of faith.

Fall (OT): refers to the disobedience of Adam and Eve (Gen. 3:1–24), the expulsion from the Garden of Eden and the resulting 'primal' or 'original sin' which has affected all of humanity.

falsification (P): to prove something to be false.

■ It is often used in reference to religious language, and is associated with Anthony Flew. We can make statements that can be proved true or false by, for example, observation ('That church has a spire'), but many philosophers have questioned whether or not statements about God (e.g. 'God is love') can be proved to be true or false, since there is a lack of empirical evidence.

fasting (OT/NT/C): to go without food as part of an ongoing act of devotion to God.

▨ It is an ancient and widespread obligation, usually accompanied by prayer, and is seen as a sign of human humility.

▨ In the Old Testament, the 'Day of *Atonement*' was a national day of fasting (Lev. 16:1–35), although the prophets warned that fasting without repentance did not bring benefit (Jer. 14:12).

In the New Testament, Jesus fasted on occasion (Matt. 4:2), the *Pharisees* fasted 2 days a week (Lk 18:12), and the early Church practised fasting (Acts 13:2). In the Christian Church, fasting is seen as a discipline designed to strengthen the spiritual life. Usually it does not involve going without food totally, but instead means going without a meal, or without meat. There are two fast days in the Roman Catholic Church: Ash Wednesday and Good Friday. In the Church of England there are no specific fast days, although many members practise fasting during Lent.

feasts (OT/NT): in biblical terms, the occasions when the Hebrews celebrated and gave thanks to God for his blessings upon them.

▨ There were three great feasts, or festivals. The *Passover* and *unleavened bread* commemorated the *Exodus* from Egypt and took place in the first month (Exod. 12). Seven weeks later, at the end of a busy agricultural season, the Feast of Weeks marked the beginning of the wheat harvest (Deut. 16). The harvest celebration, commemorating the whole Hebrew harvest, was called the Feast of *Tabernacles*, or Feast of Booths, and was held from the fifteenth to the twenty-second day of the seventh month.

fellowship (C): unity of believers, based on love, its basis being Jesus' words to his disciples in John 13 requiring them to have love for each other.

▨ In the Christian Church, the clearest example of fellowship comes with the celebration of the *Eucharist*, in which believers are able to enjoy fellowship with each other and with Christ.

Feuerbach, Ludwig (1804–72) (P): German philosopher whose most important work was ***The Essence of Christianity*** (1841), in which he argued that there is an essential difference between humans and animals.

▨ He claimed that, whereas animals are led by instinct alone, human beings have the power of thought and reflection, which allows them to understand such notions as love, kindness and sympathy. These are 'perfections', and we are thus able to see how far short we fall of them and what we ought to try to be like. To explain why we do not reach perfection, Feuerbach spoke of our 'alienation' and argued that, to get around our dilemma, we give all these human perfections to an imaginary non-human being, God. Feuerbach claimed that we make the mistake of giving our love and concern to this 'imaginary' God, when instead we should be loving our fellow humans. He claimed that all the articles of faith and the symbols of Christianity are illusory. Feuerbach suggested that once humans redirect their love and concern towards each other, then the human condition will greatly improve and the illusions of religion will vanish.

fideism (from the Latin *fides*, meaning faith) **(C/P):** the view that religious belief must be based on faith and not on reasoning or evidence.

■ Fideism argues that the fundamental claims made by religion cannot be 'proved' by scientific data or rational arguments. In its most moderate form, fideism suggests that, in establishing the 'truth' about religion, faith must come before reason. Nonetheless, reason and evidence can play a part, especially in making religious truths understandable to all. Many theologians and philosophers have been sympathetic to this view, including St *Augustine*, Pascal and Kierkegaard.

finite (P): limited in time, space, freedom and power.

Five Ks (S): five aspects of Sikh appearance for those who are initiated into the *Khalsa*, so called because they begin with the letter K.

■ The Five Ks are: (1) 'kes' — uncut hair; (2) 'kangha' — comb; (3) 'kara' — wrist band; (4) 'kirpan' — sword/dagger; (5) 'kachh' — shorts.

forgiveness (OT/NT/C): the re-establishment of a relationship after a disruption.

■ In the Old Testament, God is seen as always ready to forgive his people under the right conditions (Is. 43:1), and the system of *sacrifice* was designed as an expression of personal *repentance* which could lead to God's forgiveness being granted.

In the New Testament, God's forgiveness comes through Christ (Mk 2:10) and the Gospels teach that believers should be ready to forgive each other, whilst the Lord's Prayer suggests that God's forgiveness will be granted when believers, in their turn, forgive others. Perhaps the most famous teaching on forgiveness is the parable of the Prodigal Son (Lk 15:11–32).

form criticism (OT/NT/C): aspect of *biblical criticism* that examines the form in which the writing and the ideas contained within the Bible may have been shaped by the lifestyle of the time.

Four Noble Truths (B): essential teaching in Buddhism, the understanding of which leads towards enlightenment. It is the aim of Buddhist practice to reach such an understanding.

■ The Four Noble Truths are: (1) suffering ('*dukkha*'); (2) the cause of suffering (craving/desire); (3) the end of suffering ('*nibbana*'); (4) the way to end suffering (*Eightfold Path*). Buddhists believe that before enlightenment there can only be limited understanding of the truths but, at the moment of enlightenment, the true nature of suffering is revealed, its cause is ended, and the way ahead is fully developed.

Free Church of England/Scotland (C): small Protestant group which began after a dispute in 1843. In 1927 it was united with the Reformed Episcopal Church, a similar group from America.

■ The Free Church of Scotland was formed in 1843 by the separation of many ministers of the Church of Scotland. In 1900 it joined with the United Presbyterian Church to form the United Free Church.

free will defence (P): one possible solution to the problem of evil, which suggests that evil actions are the result of the exercise of an individual's free will and that, consequently, God cannot be held responsible.

▨ One objection to the argument is that, whilst it may account for 'moral evil' — murder, war and so on — it cannot account for 'natural or physical evil' such as earthquakes.

▨ *TIP* An important philosophical concept in questions on evil and suffering. It is integral to the theodicies of *Augustine* and *Irenaeus*.

fundamentalism (C): belief that the Bible is literally true in all respects — factual, historical and religious.

Gandhi, Mahatma (1869–1948) (H): prominent leader of Indian nationalism who championed the poor and led non-violent campaigns of protest which helped India to gain independence from Britain.

■ He was assassinated by a Hindu fanatic in Delhi in 1948.

Ganesha (H): 'Lord of Troops', Hindu deity usually depicted with an elephant's head.

■ Ganesha is the god of luck and learning, and is often invoked at the beginning of difficult tasks.

Ganga (or Ganges) **(H):** most sacred river in Hinduism. It is said to flow from the foot of *Vishnu* and through the hair of *Shiva*. Many Hindus seek to die near the river.

Gentile (OT/NT/J): term stemming from the Hebrew word *goi*, meaning a non-Jewish person.

■ In biblical times, the Jews saw themselves as God's 'Chosen People' and made a strict division between themselves and the non-Jews of other nations, whom they called 'Gentiles'.

gifts of the Spirit (NT/C): term borrowed from Paul who says, in the New Testament, that the Holy Spirit grants specific gifts to believers, not always the same gifts to every believer, but a range which, when put together, contributes to the health of the entire Christian community or 'body' (Rom. 12:3–8).

■ The gifts described include prophecy, serving others, teaching, leadership, mercy and love.

Gnosticism (from the Greek *gnosis*, meaning 'knowledge') **(C):** religious cult which flourished particularly during the first and second centuries CE.

■ Gnostics believed that humans lived in a kind of darkness and needed to achieve salvation by receiving knowledge about their true selves, their heavenly origin and their relationship with God. Human spirits were depicted as particles of light which had fallen from the 'upper world' of the spirit into the 'prisonhouse' of the material world. Those who were worthy would receive the knowledge and would then 'belong' again to the upper spiritual world. Salvation was seen as freedom from the demands of the material world. When they had acquired this, they would no longer be bound by the materialism of earthly life. The knowledge would be given to humanity by a heavenly figure or 'Redeemer'. Gnosticism was seen as a *heresy* by the early Church, although there are clear similarities between the notion of the 'Redeemer' and Jesus Christ. Indeed, some aspects of John's Gospel (e.g. Jn 1:1–18) appear to contain Gnostic elements.

Gobind Singh (1666–1708) (S): tenth and last personal *Guru* of the Sikhs.

■ In 1699, at Anandpur, he gathered the Sikhs together for the inauguration of the *Khalsa*, perhaps the most crucial event in Sikh history. After suffering attacks from Mighal enemy forces, Gobind Singh moved to the southern Punjab, where he later declared that the personal line of Gurus was to end. He conferred the authority of the Guru onto the *Adi Granth* (Guru Granth) and the Sikh community, or 'Panth'. He was assassinated in 1708.

God (Christianity) (C): creator of the universe, which is distinct from himself, but within which he remains active.

■ God's attributes include eternity, immutability (unchangingness), omnipotence (all-powerfulness) and omniscience (all-knowingness). He is depicted as a loving 'father' who offers a personal and loving relationship to all who believe in him. Although Christianity teaches monotheism — that is, that there is one God — it is a complex issue, since the 'one' God is said to have three aspects: God the Father, God the Son and God the Holy Spirit. Together, this is known as the *Trinity*.

Gospel (NT/C): Old English word meaning 'good news', which refers to the central concept of Christianity, that is, the 'good news' of salvation and redemption through Christ (Lk 4:18).

■ The word is also given to the first four books of the New Testament — Matthew, Mark, Luke and John — which tell the 'good news' of Christ.

Gotama (B): family name of the Buddha, the founder of Buddhism.

■ His personal name was Siddartha, and he was probably born around 484 BCE to a fairly wealthy family in India. He was unhappy with his wealthy lifestyle and, when he witnessed suffering in an old man, a sick man, a corpse and a wandering ascetic, he left his comfortable home at the age of 29 to become a wandering ascetic himself. After 6 years he rejected this path and sat in meditation beneath a bodhi tree at Bodhgaya, where he gained enlightenment. He taught for the next 45 years and organised the Buddhist order (*Sangha*). He died around 404 BCE.

grace (OT/NT/C): undeserved love of God which is given to humanity.

■ In the Old Testament, grace was depicted as God's kindness and love towards the people of Israel through the forgiveness of their sins (Exod. 33:19; Is. 63:9). In the New Testament, grace is linked to Christ, who represents God's love towards humanity (Jn 1:14–17). Paul believed that it was through grace that believers were called to God (Rom. 3:21–27; 1 Cor. 1:27–31) and that to live under God's grace was to live in faith and obedience (Rom. 6:1–14). In the Christian Church, there has been much controversy over the exact

g

nature of grace. The dominant thinking has been based on the view of St *Augustine*, that grace is a kind of force or power from God which supports those who are able to receive it.

Greeks (NT): in New Testament times, term for those who came from Greece as well as all those people who had a knowledge of Greek culture or who lived in the sophisticated cities of the Roman Empire.

■ It was commonly used to refer to *Gentiles* in general, and therefore references to 'Jews and Greeks' could mean the whole of humanity (Rom. 2:9–11).

Gunpowder Plot (C): failed attempt (1605) by Guy Fawkes and others to blow up the Houses of Parliament and to destroy the King in the hope that Roman Catholics would then be able to seize the government.

■ The plotters were discovered and executed.

gurdwara (S): Sikh term, meaning 'Guru's door' — local place where the Sikh scriptures are installed.

■ Every gurdwara is a place of worship and also a community centre. It should include a hospice and a refectory ('langar'), at which meals are served free to anyone who comes. The building is marked by a triangular flag ('nishan') of coloured saffron or dark blue. The person in charge is known as a 'granthi' (reader).

Gurmat (S): Sikh term, meaning 'teachings of the Guru' — refers to what in English is called 'Sikhism'.

■ The sources of Gurmat are the scriptures, principally the *Adi Granth* and the tradition, not accepted by all Sikhs, of initiation into the *Khalsa*.

Guru (S): Hindi term for religious teacher or leader, with particular significance for the Sikh religion, whose doctrines derive from a succession of ten Gurus who taught in the Punjab in the sixteenth and seventeenth centuries.

■ The Ten Gurus were *Nanak*, Angad, Amar Das, Ram Das, Arjan, Hargobind, Hari Rai, Hari Krishan, Tegh Bahadur and Gobind Singh.

Guru Granth Sahib (S): principal Sikh scripture, originally called the 'Granth Sahib' ('Revered Book'), but named the Guru Granth Sahib after the line of personal *Gurus* ended in 1708.

■ The scriptures offer a message of spiritual liberation through belief in the divine name ('*Nam*'). It is also known as the '*Adi Granth*'.

Guru Nanak (c. 1469–1539 CE) (S): first *Guru* of Sikhism and the founder of the faith.

■ After spending his childhood in the Punjabi village of Talvandi, he had a vision commanding him to give up everything and to preach the '*Nam*'. He preached throughout India before settling in Kartarpur to guide his followers in their search for enlightenment. He was succeeded by his disciple, Guru Angad.

Hades (OT/NT/J): in the Old Testament, a shadowy place where the dead dwelt, awaiting judgement (Eccles. 9:3).

■ It is not a place of torment, but rather more of distress (Ps. 88:3). In the New Testament, there are references to pain for unrepentant sinners (Mk 9:45). In the Book of Revelation, Christ is said to have possession of the keys of Hades (Rev. 1:18) and that, at the very end, the dead will rise from Hades with the establishment of the reign of God.

Hadith (I): body of traditions in Islam, comprising the sayings of Muhammad, his Companions and other prominent early Muslims, and the guidance necessary for law and life, second only to the Qur'an.

■ Originally there were thousands of individual sayings and, in the ninth century CE, these were finally reduced to smaller collections of 4,000 hadiths, called 'the two Sahihs'. Four more collections were later added.

hajj (I): Islamic pilgrimage and one of the *Pillars of Islam*.

■ Every adult Muslim should perform a pilgrimage to Mecca and the shrine of *Ka'ba* at least once in his or her lifetime. During the pilgrimage, the pilgrim wears a ritually clean garb called 'ihram' and observes certain restrictions ('tabus').

Halakhah (J): that part of traditional Jewish literature concerned with Jewish law and ritual.

■ The term 'Halakhah' is used in the *Talmud* and in the *Midrash*.

Hanuman (H): Hindu monkey-god, son of Vayu.

■ In art, he is depicted as a monkey with a partly human body and a long tail. He is particularly noted for his devotion to *Rama* and Sita.

Hare, Richard (1919 –) (E): moral philosopher who suggested that moral thinking occurs at two different levels: a lower intuitive level and a higher, more thoughtful one.

■ The lower, intuitive level is where we simply apply moral principles which we have learned without questioning. The higher level is where we think more deeply about our moral principles — believing we should only apply them if we are going to be consistent, that is, by treating all others on equal terms with ourselves. Hare is also well known for his views on *bliks* — beliefs which cannot be proved to be either true or false, yet which can nevertheless affect our actions. His works include *The Language of Morals* (1952) and *Moral Thinking* (1981). He taught at Oxford and Florida.

Harimandir Sahib (S): principal centre of Sikh devotion, located in Amritsar, India.

■ It was founded by Guru Ram Das (fourth of the Ten *Gurus*) and completed by his successor, Arjan, in the late sixteenth century. In 1984, its surroundings were badly damaged when the Indian Army launched an attack against Sikh militants who were waiting there.

■ *TIP* The Harimandir Sahib is known in the West as the 'Golden Temple', since it was covered in gilding by Maharaja Ranjit Singh in the nineteenth century.

heaven (OT/NT): in the Bible, the term has two meanings: (1) the sky; and (2) the dwelling place of God.

■ It has its first meaning in Genesis 1:1, in which God creates 'the heavens and the earth', and later the stars are said to be suspended from heaven (Job 22:12). In Isaiah 24:21–23, there is also the suggestion that the heavens will be destroyed along with the earth at the end of time. In its second meaning, it is where, for example, the throne of God is (Is. 66:1) and where the *Son of Man* sits at the right hand of the Father (Mk 14:62). In the New Testament, it is depicted as a place of joy and peace (Lk 15:7) and eternal life (Rev. 21:1–4).

hedonic calculus (E): method of working out the sum total of pleasure and pain produced by an act, outlined by Jeremy *Bentham*.

■ The calculus is described by Bentham in his book *An Introduction to the Principles of Morals and Legislation* (1789). Put simply, in order to decide what action is right in a given situation, a person should calculate the pleasure and pain which would result, using the categories of intensity, duration, certainty, propinquity, fecundity (pleasure leading to more pleasure, pain to more pain), purity (pleasure followed by pain) and extent (number of people affected). Having done this, the person then considers the merits of different courses of action in the same way. Eventually, the calculus will show which action is right. Bentham believed that the hedonic calculus would be particularly useful in criminal law reform, where it would be possible to work out the correct levels of punishment to prevent criminals from reoffending.

■ *TIP* A very important concept which is integral to questions on *utilitarianism*.

hedonism (from the Greek *hedone*, meaning 'pleasure') **(E):** belief that pleasure is the highest good and that only pleasure has value in itself, a view supported by the philosophers Epicurus and *Bentham*, amongst others.

■ The 'paradox of hedonism' was outlined by Sidgwick in *The Methods of Ethics* (1874), where it was suggested that the urge to seek pleasure can be self-defeating, since we often fail to receive pleasure if we deliberately seek it, since pleasure is not the same as happiness.

'Hedonist' is often used to describe someone who is devoted to pleasure-seeking.

h

Hellenists (NT): title given to those Jews who, in biblical times, spoke Greek rather than Aramaic and who were influenced by Greek culture and were inclined to interpret the Law of Moses less strictly than other Jews (Acts 6).

■ There were large settlements of Hellenistic Jews in Alexandria, Antioch and elsewhere in the Roman Empire. The Hellenists were a powerful influence as the early Church spread beyond Jerusalem into the Greek-speaking *Gentile* world.

henotheism (P): belief that there may be many gods, but restricting worship to only one of them.

Henry VIII (1491–1547) (C): King of England 1509–47. He opposed the Reforming movement and in 1521 took the title 'Defender of the Faith'.

■ When the Church failed to allow the dissolution of his marriage to Catherine of Aragon, he repudiated papal authority and summoned Parliament to pass an Act which would make him head of the Church of England. In 1533 Henry was excommunicated by Pope Clement VII, following Henry's marriage to Anne Boleyn. In 1534 Parliament passed a number of Acts which severed financial, judicial and administrative links with Rome.

heresy (C): formal denial or doubt of any defined doctrine of faith in the Christian Church.

■ 'Formal heresy' is the wilful following of an 'error' of faith by someone who has been baptised, and this can be seen as a grave sin involving excommunication from the Roman Catholic Church. 'Material heresy' means the holding of heretical doctrines but in 'good faith', and this is not seen as a sin.

hermeneutics (from the Greek term *hermeneuein*, meaning 'to interpret') **(C):** theory that, with the use of an interpreter and other aids ('exegesis'), a modern reader can 're-experience' the mental processes of the text's author and so be able to gain a greater understanding of the meaning of the text.

■ It stems from the notion that it is difficult for a person from one culture and time period to understand the original meaning of texts produced in a different culture (for instance, a modern Christian in the West trying to understand the Gospel accounts of Christ, which were written in a different culture).

heteronomy (E): term used by *Kant* in his *Critique of Practical Reason* (1788) to refer to actions which are undertaken as a result of fear of losing out, or for hope of a benefit which may be right, but which, in some way, lacks moral worth.

High Places (OT): in the Old Testament, areas where sacrifices were offered in the open air.

■ The prophets tended to dislike them because they were seen as part of the fertility religion of the Canaanites and were therefore incompatible with the worship of God (Hos. 4:13).

They were popular with many people, and some were apparently made 'acceptable' when used by famous biblical characters, such as Jacob at Bethel (Gen. 28:18) and Joshua and Gilgal (Josh. 4:20). The High Places were destroyed by King Josiah (2 Kgs 23:8–9).

High Priest (OT/NT): person who spoke to God on behalf of the people of Israel and who spoke on behalf of God to them.

■ The first holder of such an office was Moses' brother, Aaron.

In New Testament times, the High Priest did not hold the job for life. For example, Annas held the post from 6 to 15 CE. At the times of the trial of Jesus, the High Priest was Annas' son-in-law, Caiaphas.

Hinduism (H): name given to the religious tradition that has evolved in India over the last 3,000 years.

■ Hinduism is a diverse faith — there is no 'founder', nor any single creed, scripture, moral code or central concept of God. Rather, it is a tradition which embraces a wide range of diverse religious positions. Hinduism does, however, have some presuppositions which constitute a broad framework. These include *dhamma*, the way things truly are; Varnashrama Dharma, which is the proper observance of rules and customs; *samsara*, the cycle of birth and death; *karma*, which is the doctrine that every action produces its own inevitable result, leading to good or bad merit; *Brahman*, the impersonal absolute which underlies the diversity of the universe; and *atman*, which is the individual soul. The two best-known scriptures are the *Upanishads* and the epics of Ramayana and the *Mahabharata*.

holiness (OT/NT): that which is set aside from the world of the profane.

■ In the Old Testament, God is referred to as 'holy' and this holiness extends to his priests (Lev. 21:6).

In the New Testament, holiness is seen as a quality of both Jesus (Lk 1:35) and of Christian believers (1 Cor. 3:16).

Holy Spirit (OT/NT/C): in Christianity, part of the Trinity along with God the Father and God the Son.

■ In the Old Testament, the 'Spirit' of God is seen as the power by which God creates the universe, and the Greek word **pneuma** and the Hebrew word **ruach** are used to mean the 'breath' of God, the unseen creative force. In the New Testament, the Holy Spirit is involved in the birth of Jesus and in his baptism (Mk 1:10; Lk 3:22) and during the ministry of Jesus himself (Matt. 12:18). In John's Gospel, the Spirit is called the *Paraclete*, meaning 'defending counsel'; it helps the *Apostles* to understand the truth concerning Christ. After Jesus' resurrection, the Holy Spirit comes upon the Apostles at Pentecost (Acts 2:4) and works through the early Church, the Apostles and early believers. Many are given special *'gifts of the Spirit'* for the service of the Church (1 Cor. 12:4).

Hosea (OT): prophet from the northern kingdom of Israel at around 745 BCE. His messages were concerned with God's judgement of Israel and were based on his real-life family relationships.

■ The Book of Hosea shows the prophet speaking out against the religious, political and social life of Israel and its idolatry and injustices. His message is one of repentance and the coming of divine punishment. With it comes a message of future hope and God's unending love for his people.

h

■ *TIP* A very important prophet in examinations. Questions usually centre around God's judgement and future hope. There may be questions which refer to Hosea's family and their connection with his prophetic messages.

Hubmaier, Balthasar (c.1485–1528) (C): German *Anabaptist*.

■ In 1521 he became parish priest at Waldshut, and 2 years later he introduced the *Reformation*. However, in 1525 he gave up his support for *Zwingli*'s doctrines and turned instead to the Anabaptists. He later became involved in the Peasants' War, and some scholars suggest that he may have been the author of the 'Twelve Articles', a charter of the peasants' demands, which included the right to appoint their own pastors. He was burnt at the stake at Vienna.

humanism (E): non-religious world-view, based on the notion that human beings are autonomous and capable of self-determination, with the capacity, without religion, to improve themselves.

Hume, David (1711–76) (P): Scottish empiricist philosopher.

■ Hume's underlying philosophical aim was to show that humans are part of the natural order and that we are creatures of instinct and habit whose mental lives are driven by emotions rather than reason. He argued that religious and moral beliefs are formed by custom and habit rather than by reasoning things out. He claimed that our emotions or passions are what drive us into action and that our reason operates to support them. In this respect, he gives human reason a much lesser role than many other empiricists. In religion, he argued that religious beliefs, such as belief in *miracles*, come from our natural desire to 'blame' natural problems on invisible forces, rather than to examine the problems rationally or scientifically. He is most famous for works such as *An Enquiry Concerning Human Understanding* (1748), *The Natural History of Religion* (1757) and *Dialogues Concerning Natural Religion* (1779).

hypothetical imperative (E): term used in *Kant*'s ethics to describe an 'ought statement', which is one describing an action that is needed to achieve a certain result and which is only valid if that end is achieved by the person doing that action.

■ For example, the statement 'You ought to practise your goalkeeping' is made on the assumption that you wish to improve your goalkeeping skills and that practice will help. If, in fact, you do not wish to be a goalkeeper, then the reason for accepting the ought statement is removed. Kant suggested that moral statements are not hypothetical imperatives, since people should apply moral principles regardless of whether the person desires the result they produce.

icon (from the Greek, meaning 'image') **(C):** refers particularly to the painted or mosaic panels which depict holy persons or sacred events in Byzantine worship.

▓ Such images are seen as a testimony to the reality of Christ's *incarnation* as human and divine, and also offer a material vision of spiritual reality. Icons are also important for their representation of history, doctrine and morality.

Id (I): Islamic term for 'religious festival'.

▓ It is most often used in reference to the two great festivals — 'Id al-Adha' (sacrifice), which is associated with Abraham's intended sacrifice of his son, Isaac, and 'Id al-Fitr' (breaking the fast), which falls at the end of Ramadan, the month of fasting. Both festivals are occasions of great public celebration.

idolatry (OT/NT): cult or belief centring on a statue of a god or goddess, common in biblical times.

▓ Worshipping idols was strictly forbidden in the *Ten Commandments* ('You shall not make for yourself an idol' — Exod. 20:4), and there are incidents mentioned in the Old Testament of conflict between the faith of Israel and the idol-worshipping of other belief systems — for instance, the making of the Golden Calf (Exod. 32:4) and the contest on Mount Carmel between Elijah and the prophets of Baal (1 Kgs 18:16–40). In the New Testament, Paul warns the Christians in Corinth about some of their civic ceremonies which contain elements of idolatry (1 Cor. 10:14).

Ignatius Loyola (c.1491–1556) (C): founder of the Jesuits and probable writer of *Spiritual Exercises*.

▓ In 1554 he and six companions made a vow of poverty, chastity and of a pilgrimage to Rome, to be followed by a life of devotion to working for Christ. In 1537 they offered their services to the Pope, and in 1540 the Society of Jesus was solemnly sanctioned. Ignatius became the first general.

Imam (I): Islamic term meaning 'exemplar model', most commonly used to refer to the leader of Muslim worship in the mosque, but also referring to the charismatic leaders of the *Shi'ah* sect of Islam, who claim that God has designated a line of members of the family of 'Ali to act as spiritual and secular guides for the community.

▓ The Imam (leader of mosque worship) may be any adult male Muslim of good character in the community, and need not be an ordained priest.

In Shi'ism, the last member of the Imam line disappeared in the ninth century, and the Shi'ah now await the return of the expected Imam, the *Mahdi*, who will re-establish a reign of peace and justice on earth.

iman (I): 'faith' in Islam, which is required for salvation and usually comprises three elements: (1) intention ('niyya'); (2)profession ('qual'); and (3) works ('amal').

immortality (P): term meaning endless life or existence.

immutable (P): term, when used to refer to God, meaning unchanging and unchangeable.

incarnation (NT): term meaning 'becoming flesh' or 'becoming human'.

■ Although the term is not used in the Bible, scholars use it to refer to Christ being both divine and yet 'becoming flesh' on earth. For example, in John's Gospel he refers to the Word becoming flesh (Jn 1:14) and that Jesus had come from God (Jn 10:38), yet that he also had human qualities, such as weeping (Jn 11:35), and that he died (Jn 19:30).

In Hinduism, the term *'avatar'* is used for the incarnation of a god.

in continuo (P): when referring to God, term meaning 'continuing to act in the world'.

■ It is used when talking about how God has created the world and still acts within it.

ineffable (P): used to refer to the qualities of God which are beyond human words.

infinite (P): term meaning 'without limitations of time, space, knowledge, freedom or power'.

in intellectu (P): philosophical term meaning 'in the mind', used in the *ontological argument* to claim that God's existence must be more than in the mind — he must exist in reality as well.

in re (P): philosophical term meaning 'in reality'.

insan (from the Arabic for 'man') **(I):** Islamic doctrine of man.

■ The Qur'an sees humanity as God's great creation, created from clay as his representation on earth and to serve and glorify him. Humans have a soul ('ruh'), which returns to God when the body dies.

intuitionism (E): theory of moral knowledge which suggests that we know the rightness or wrongness of certain actions through our own sense of 'intuition'.

■ It was most popularly advocated by G. E. Moore in ***Principia Ethica*** (1903).

Irenaeus, St (c. 130–200 CE) (P): first great Catholic theologian.

■ His most famous work, ***Against Heresies***, was a treatise against what he regarded as the false teaching of *Gnosticism*. His writings led to the development of the concept of Irenaean Theodicy.

■ *TIP* An important theologian — can be relevant to questions of 'evil and suffering' and those concerning the authorship of the Fourth Gospel.

Isaiah (OT): eighth-century BCE prophet, often associated with Jerusalem.

■ He advised four different kings of Judah between 740 and 701 BCE, at a time when there was a serious threat from the invading Assyrians. The Book of Isaiah in the Old Testament is not a single book, and is probably best understood if seen in two or even three parts: chapters 1–39, 40–55 and 56–66. 'First Isaiah' refers to the prophet who lived in court circles, and is concerned with two major political dramas — the first, where Judah's neighbours tried to force it into an alliance against Assyria, and the second, the Assyrian threat to Jerusalem. In the first drama, Isaiah tries and fails to warn the King, Ahaz, not to join the alliance against Assyria (Is. 1–9) and in the second, Isaiah prophesies that the King's lack of faith in God, together with the social wrongs of the country, will lead to God punishing the people with war. Ahaz's successor, Hezekiah, finally frees the people from the Assyrian threat and removes all foreign idols. 'Second Isaiah' is concerned with the *Exile* and captivity of the people of Israel in Babylon. The prophet's message is that God will one day bring salvation.

Islam (meaning 'submission [to God]') **(I):** monotheistic religion, founded by the prophet Muhammad in the seventh century CE, whose sacred book is the Qur'an.

▓ Followers of Islam are called Muslims — a Muslim is 'one who submits himself to God' (*Allah*) — and they regard Islam as the final unfolding of God's revelation to humanity and the complete system of faith and behaviour.

Israel (J): country in the Middle East, the modern Jewish state founded on the ancient 'Holy Land' of Judaism in May 1948.

▓ The United Nations partition plan of 1947 tried to create two states, one Arab and one Jewish, in what was then called Palestine, but the Arabs refused to accept the existence of a separate Jewish state and declared war in 1948. An armistice followed in 1949, but a state of war and unrest existed between Israel and its Arab neighbours until Egypt signed the Camp David peace treaty with Israel in 1977. Peace with Jordan followed with the signing of the treaty with the Palestine Liberation Organisation in 1994.

Jehovah (OT): term used in English to refer to the name of God.

▓ To the Hebrews, the divine name of God was YHWH and was deemed to be so sacred that the word was never pronounced. Instead, the Jews used the word 'Adonai' ('Lord'). When vowels were added to the Hebrew script, the vowels inserted into YHWH were those of Adonai, producing the form 'Jehovah', which has been used in several versions of the English Bible.

Jeremiah (OT): one of the major prophets of Judah.

▓ He began his work in 626 BCE and prophesied under five different kings, ending with the fall of Jerusalem in 587 BCE. He came from a priestly family and for 40 years continually warned his people that God's judgement would come upon them because of their sin. He was unpopular because he urged the people not to resist the Babylonians when they invaded. In 587 BCE the Babylonians under Nebuchadnezzar destroyed Jerusalem and the *Temple*, and the people of Judah were taken into exile. The Book of Jeremiah is one of the three great prophetical books of the Old Testament. It contains a wide range of writing — poetry, prose, parables and history. Jeremiah is generally seen as a prophet who brought a message of despair but also of hope, for he promised that God would one day restore the people to their homeland and make a 'new *covenant*' with them.

▓ **TIP** Questions on Jeremiah often examine the material in chapters 29–31, which deal with the new covenant.

Jerusalem (OT/NT/J/I): capital of Israel, located in the Judean hills in the southern biblical kingdom of Judah.

▓ It has existed since at least 1800 BCE, and King David brought the *Ark* of the Covenant there and made the city his capital. His son, Solomon, built the *Temple*, and Jerusalem became the 'Holy City'. It was attacked by enemies several times — in 587–86 BCE the Babylonians destroyed both the city and the Temple, and 500 years later the Romans took control and King Herod restored the city, which was visited several times by Jesus. The early Christian Church spread out from its centre in Jerusalem. In 70 CE, following a revolt by a Jewish force, the Romans destroyed the city's defences and the Temple. In the fourth century CE the city became Christian. The city came under Islamic

j

control in 637 CE and remained that way for most of the time up to 1948 CE, when the state of Israel was created and the city was divided between the Jews and the Arabs. In 1967 the Jews won control of the entire city. To Muslims, Jerusalem is the third most sacred city after Mecca and Medina, and the Qur'an tells of Muhammad's journey to what has been identified as the site of Solomon's temple. In 691 CE the Muslims built the 'Dome of the Rock' on the site, and today Muslims are encouraged to make a pilgrimage to the site.

Jesus (NT/C/I): principal figure in the Christian religion. The name 'Jesus' comes from the common Jewish name 'Joshua', which means 'He whose salvation is God'.

He was born in Bethlehem c. 6 BCE and from the age of about 30 preached to the people of Israel. He is said to have performed many miracles and to have preached about the *'kingdom of God'*. His mission was to show that God is loving and near, and that those who turn to him (repent) will receive salvation. His mission lasted about 3 years, but the Jewish religious authorities were afraid of his power and of his claim to be able to forgive sin — something only God could do. Eventually they had him arrested, and he was crucified by the Roman authorities. It is claimed that Jesus rose from the dead on the third day and that his people saw and heard him for 40 days afterwards, apparently proving his claim to be the *Son of God*. His story is told in all four Gospels. In Christianity, Jesus is the central figure — he is seen as the Son of God, who is the 'saviour' of all, and that those who accept him will be free from the power of sin and will be able to enter into eternal life.

In Islam, Jesus is called 'Isa' and is seen as a messenger and a prophet, though not the Son of God.

jihad (Arabic for 'conflict') **(I):** Islamic term for 'holy war' — that is, war against unbelievers.

It is one of the five *Pillars* of Islam. Behind jihad is the notion that Islam is a universal position and that force may be used to spread its message. Jihad has sometimes been interpreted as warfare for the defence of Islam and as a spiritual struggle against the evil inside oneself.

Job (OT): fictional character in the Old Testament about whom the Book of Job is written.

Job is depicted as a good, righteous man who meets with disaster — he loses his children and his wealth and contracts a hideous disease. His friends, in their efforts to comfort him, tell him that he must have sinned against God to have brought upon himself such suffering. Job cannot understand how God can allow a good man to suffer in this way. Finally, God himself speaks to Job and Job understands that God is much bigger than the religious thinking of the day could comprehend. The story ends with Job restored. The Book of Job is unique in the Old Testament — the author is unknown, and we do not know when it was written; the beginning and the end are prose and the rest is in poetry.

John the Apostle (NT): disciple of Jesus and the brother of James and son of Zebedee.

■ He was a fisherman and close to Jesus. He was present at the raising of Jairus' daughter (Lk 8:5), at the *Transfiguration* (Lk 9:28) and in the Garden of Gethsemane (Mk 14:33). He was a key member of the early Church and is, possibly, the author of John's Gospel (the Fourth Gospel). There is a tradition that he died in Ephesus at an old age.

John the Baptist (NT): son of Elizabeth and Zechariah (Lk 1:5–25), depicted as the prophet sent by God to prepare the people for the coming of Jesus (Lk 3:1–20).

■ He lived in the desert, dressed in animal skins, and called on the people to repent and to be baptised in the River Jordan. He baptised Jesus himself, who later declared: 'among those born of women there is no one greater than John' (Lk 7:28). He spoke out against King Herod Antipas' marriage and was subsequently beheaded.

Jonah (OT): Hebrew prophet, possibly dating from c. 600 BCE.

■ Jonah appears in the Book of Jonah in the Old Testament. He is called by God to give a message to the citizens of an enemy city called Nineveh. He is to warn them of God's coming judgement of them. Jonah does not want to do this and tries to run away from God. In trying to flee, he is thrown overboard from a ship and is swallowed by a great fish and taken back to dry land. Reluctantly, Jonah goes to Nineveh and delivers the message. The people of Nineveh change their ways and God shows mercy on them, much to Jonah's annoyance. The story of Jonah highlights the love and compassion of God for all people.

Judaism (J): religion of the Jewish people.

■ Judaism dates back to the destruction of the *Temple* in 70 CE, which distinguishes it from the religion of the biblical period. After 70 CE, Judaism emphasises the religion of the home and the synagogue, and includes the development of councils of sages and the role of the Rabbi as teacher and authority. The main ideas of Judaism centre around the concept of teachings stemming from God — the *Torah*, oral teachings and *Midrash*. God's commandments are contained in the Torah and enter into every aspect of Jewish life. Judaism is a monotheistic faith, coupled with the belief that a *Messiah* will come and bring in a new age.

Judgement Day (OT/NT): in the Old Testament, God is sometimes depicted as a judge who will reward people according to their deeds — anger on the evil and blessings on the righteous (Deut. 10:12–22). The prophets Amos and Joel both said that there would be a day of judgement, when people would be punished unless they repented.

■ A day of judgement is also mentioned in the New Testament; in John's Gospel, there is the suggestion that judgement is already taking place (Jn 9:39), whilst Paul speaks of a future judgement in which the evil and the righteous will be separated for ever (Rom. 2:1–4) and where Christ would judge the world.

justification (from the Latin *justum facere*, meaning 'to make just') **(C):** used particularly in Protestant theology to highlight an act where God, by virtue of the sacrifice of Christ, forgives someone the punishment they are due because of their sins.

■ Martin *Luther* said that such justification was granted to people as a result of their faith.

Ka'ba (I): most holy shrine in Islam, regarded as the House of God.

▨ Situated in Mecca, it is cube-shaped and resides in a sacred enclosure called the Haram, from which unbelievers are excluded. It is said to date back from the time of Abraham and was made the focal point of Islam by Muhammad. In the eastern corner is the 'Black Stone', which is a special object of veneration, and pilgrims walk around it in a ritual way.

The pilgrimage to Mecca and the Ka'ba (*hajj*) is one of the five *Pillars of Islam*.

Kabbalah (J): form of Jewish mysticism.

▨ The main text of the Kabbalah is the 'Zohar', which originates from the thirteenth century. The Kabbalah teaches that the creation of the world took place through a series of emanations from God. These emanatory structures, called the ten 'sefirot', are the inner construction of all reality and divine manifestations, and represent a balance of harmony and divine energy which sustain humanity and nature. Sin affects this harmony and allows evil to become active. The Kabbalah has led to the growth of several mystic messianic movements.

Kali (meaning 'black') **(H):** Hindu goddess who came into being on a battlefield in order to destroy an army of demons ('asuras') by eating them and drinking their blood.

▨ In art she is shown as black or dark blue, with a necklace of corpses and severed heads. Her most famous temple is at Kalighat in Calcutta.

Kama (H): Hindu god of love who, with *artha, dharma* and *moksha*, makes up the four goals of life in the Hindu tradition.

▨ Kama actually represents the pursuit of love and pleasure, and relates closely to the way of life of the married householder.

Kant, Immanuel (1724–1804) (P/E): one of the most influential philosophers of modern times.

▨ He was born in East Prussia (in Germany), and spent the main part of his career as Chair of Philosophy at the University of Königsberg.

Kant's philosophy can be best seen as attempting to answer three questions — 'What can I know?', 'What ought I to do?' and 'What can I hope for?' In his ***Critique of Pure Reason*** (1781), he tried to show that it is impossible to know anything about the world without using our cognitive principles, and that traditional 'proofs' of God are unsound because they do not establish knowledge in any true sense. He claimed that metaphysical 'proofs' are expressions of interest only, but that there are certain questions which simply cannot be answered. In particular, he said that questions about God, freedom and immortality can only be answered through faith.

In the field of ethics, Kant suggested that freedom and morality give us cause to believe in the reality of God and eternal life. He argued that, if humans are to act as moral beings, then there must be God and eternal life, since without them there would be moral despair. Moral action ought to lead to happiness and so, if this cannot be achieved in this life, then it must be achieved with God in the hereafter. To realise what Kant called the 'summum bonum' or 'highest good' will require this. Belief in God and eternal life are, according to Kant, central to 'moral faith'.

karma (meaning 'deed' or 'work') **(H/B)**: central concept in both Hinduism and Buddhism.

■ Karma is an intentional action carried out by a person, and such actions will eventually determine the future of that individual and their future reincarnation. Thus, certain powerful acts of positive merit, such as worship and pilgrimage, will lead to 'good' karma and the wiping out of 'bad' karma.

kashrut **(J)**: general term for Jewish dietary requirements.

■ In Judaism, certain foods are forbidden, whilst others are 'kosher' — fit to eat. Food which meets the dietary requirements includes animals which chew the cud and have cloven hoofs (e.g. cattle); birds which are not birds of prey; and fish with scales. Before eating, the animals have to be ritually slaughtered and all the blood removed.

kerygma (from the Greek for 'proclamation') **(NT)**: those parts of the New Testament which are deemed by scholars to be 'preaching' material rather than historical or descriptive material, 'proclaiming' the redemptive work of Jesus and the fulfilment of Old Testament prophecy.

■ Examples include Luke 11 and 1 Corinthians 1.

khalq **(I)**: Islamic idea of creation, in which God, who is pre-existing and eternal, creates the world out of nothing but himself ('ex nihilo') in 6 days.

Khalsa **(S)**: Sikh order established by Guru *Gobind Singh* in 1699, giving the Sikhs a visible identity or brotherhood.

■ Entry into the Khalsa is through an initiation rite ('amrit sanskar'), in which five devout Sikhs administer baptism using sweet water stirred by a sword ('khande di pahul'). Those who join the Khalsa must live according to the Khalsa code ('Rahit'). Male members of the Khalsa add 'Singh' to their names. Females add 'Kaur'.

kingdom of God **(NT)**: one of the most important themes in the teaching of Christ, it has two meanings: (1) a future promise (linked to the coming of the Messiah) that one day God's kingdom will be established and that evil will be vanquished; (2) a present reality, that God's kingdom is already here, as demonstrated in the life and work of Christ.

■ Jesus seemed to teach about the kingdom of God in both ways; the presence of God's rule was seen through his miracles (Lk 11:20), yet in many of the *parables*, Jesus said that the kingdom had, in a sense, arrived. He seemed to be suggesting that although the kingdom was present, it would not really be established until his return and the coming of the new age. The Jews thought that the kingdom of God was going to mean freedom from the Romans, but Jesus made it clear that it would come only with slow growth, which would eventually change the whole world.

■ *TIP* This topic is popular with examiners. Questions often revolve around the views of scholars concerning what Jesus might have meant in his teachings on the kingdom of God — particularly as to whether the kingdom was coming in the future or was already present in Jesus. Useful passages include Luke 6–9, 13–15 and John 3.

Krishna (H): an *avatar* of *Vishnu* and a divine hero in the *Mahabharata*. In the *Bhagavad Gita*, his teachings are developed as he takes on the role of charioteer for his friend Arjuna.

■ In art he is blue in colour and dressed in yellow, with peacock feathers in his crown. In northern India he is worshipped as Radha-Krishna with his lover Radha.

Kshatriya (H): name given to one of the four classes (*varnas*) in Hindu society. The Kshatriyas are the rulers and warriors, and are generally seen to be second in prominence after the *Brahmans*.

Lamb of God (NT): title used by John the Baptist to refer to Jesus (Jn 1:29). It also occurs in Revelation 5:6 as a description of Christ slain as a ransom for sin.

■ It is thought to be linked to the fact that Jesus' death occurred at the time of the slaughter of the *Passover* lambs in the *Temple*.

language games (P): concept developed by the Austrian philosopher Ludwig *Wittgenstein* (1889–1951).

■ In his work *Philosophical Investigations* (1953), Wittgenstein spoke of 'language games', by which he was suggesting that language is like a game we play. There are many different games, and each has its own rules; it does not make sense to take the rules of one game and apply them to another. In the same way, language is used by different people in different contexts and, in a sense, there are many different 'language games' that go on. The meaning of a word in a particular 'game' (or context) is determined by the 'rules' of that game, i.e. by the way the word is used. Thus, for Wittgenstein, language games highlight the fact that religious language is used in the 'religious language game' and therefore is best understood by those who are actually playing that language game as well.

language, religious (P): statements about God, religious belief and ways of life.

■ Some philosophers argue that religious language is a distinctive form of language that can only be used in reference to the religious 'form of life', and that in other contexts, religious language may be meaningless. Others have argued that religious language is meaningless anyway, because its truth or falsity cannot be proved.

■ *TIP* A very important topic in philosophy of religion examinations. Questions may be asked on analogy, myth, symbol, language games and the verification and falsification debates.

Laud, William (1573–1645) (C): Archbishop of Canterbury from 1633, who opposed the moves towards Calvinist theology and tried to restore traditional liturgical practices into the Church of England.

■ He received bitter criticism from many quarters, particularly the Puritans, who objected to his attempts to impose liturgical uniformity. In 1640 he compelled many groups of people to swear never to allow the government of the Church to be changed — the so-called 'etcetera oath'. Soon after this, however, Laud was impeached by the Long Parliament and was executed in 1645.

Law (OT/NT): English translation of the Hebrew word '*Torah*' and used in the Old Testament to refer to the Pentateuch, the first five books of the Bible in which the Law is contained.

■ In biblical times, 'law', as in the administration of justice, was often carried out by elders who sat at the city gates, whilst more difficult cases might be decided in the *Temple*, or by the King himself.

Within the Pentateuch there are several legal codes. The oldest is the Covenant Code (Exod. 21:1–21), which gives rules concerning slavery, murder and theft. The Priestly Code is concerned with religious rituals, and the Deuteronomic Code (Deut. 12–26) makes obedience to the Law a condition of the *covenant*. After the *Exile*, the Law became increasingly elaborate, and the oral Law was collected together to form the *Mishnah*.

In his teachings, and particularly in the *Sermon on the Mount* (Matt. 5–7), Jesus gave much of the Law a radical new interpretation.

legalism (E): where the correctness of a moral act is decided not by reference to the motive of the person carrying it out, but by its conformity to a moral rule.

■ It sees morality rather like a legal code, with set rules of conduct, backed by punishments and sanctions.

Levites (OT): one of the 12 *tribes of Israel*, stemming from Levi, Jacob's son.

■ Originally, the Levites were designated to be the priests of the Hebrews, with responsibility for offering sacrifices and teaching the *Law* (Deut. 17:9). After the *Exile*, however, they were only allotted minor duties in the *Temple*.

■ *TIP* In the Old Testament, the term 'Levite' and 'Priest' are often interchangeable.

liberalism (C): non-fundamental interpretation of the Bible or Christian doctrine.

■ For example, it may be used to refer to the idea that Jesus was not actually the Son of God, but that he was a 'special' man who was invested with God's power.

liberation theology (C): movement based on the view that the poor and oppressed of the developing world must be encouraged to liberate themselves, rather than remain dependent on outside aid.

■ It became popular in Latin America in the late 1960s and early 1970s, and owed much to the *Second Vatican Council* and the decision by the Latin American Episcopal Conference in 1968 to opt for a liberation model of development. The biblical basis for the view comes from the example of the Israelites under Moses, who refused to accept slavery in Egypt, and by the teachings of Christ, who was on the side of the poor against the exploitation of the rich (e.g. Lk 16). In some countries — for instance Brazil, Peru and Central America — the Bible has been used to justify political action by the poor against those in power. Liberation theology has been criticised by some for its apparent Marxist views and lack of critical scholarship.

The most famous text is *A Theology of Liberation* (1971) by Gustayo Gutierrez.

Liturgical Movement (C): Roman Catholic movement in the 1900s which tried to encourage congregations to participate in the *Mass.*

■ It led to more frequent and simplified services.

liturgy (meaning 'work of the people') **(C):** refers to the part of a Christian service of worship in which the congregation participates in word or action, normally by following a set form of service — for example the Roman Missal, the Book of Common Prayer or the Alternative Service Book.

logical impossibility (P): something which is impossible because it defies reason, for instance a square circle.

■ In religion, some philosophers have argued that the notion of God is a logical impossibility because God's characteristics are so far removed from reason — for instance, he is said to be timeless, yet acts within time.

logical necessity (P): view that something must be the case.

■ In philosophy of religion this may be used, for example, in the argument that evil is necessary in the world for the existence of good.

logical positivism (P): school of thought which argues that something that cannot be verified or falsified (proved to be true or false) by use of sense experience (seeing, hearing, touching etc.) or by mathematics or logic is meaningless.

■ Supporters of logical positivism argue that religious language is meaningless.

logos (NT): Greek noun meaning 'word'.

■ In John 1:1, the 'Word' is said to be God and with God, and through the Word, creation came about. The author brings from Judaism the idea of God's breath (*ruah*), from which creation comes — just as, in Genesis 1:3, God creates the world by speaking ('God said...'). Moreover, for Jews, the 'Word' of God incorporated his wisdom, embodied in the *Law* — in a sense, the Word gave meaning to life. He goes further by suggesting that Jesus is the Word in human form and was with God from the beginning and was the agent of creation — the way in which God's life was imparted into humanity (Jn 1:1–14). The Word is a living and distinct person within the *Trinity*, and the source of true light. Without the Word, there is darkness. Later, in Revelation 19:13, Jesus is identified as the 'Word of God', or the 'Word made flesh'.

■ *TIP* A very important concept — make sure that you understand the importance of God's creating power through his 'Word', and how the 'Word' is identified in Christianity with Jesus. John 1:1–18 are most important.

Lord's Prayer (NT/C): name given to the prayer that Jesus taught his disciples (Matt. 6:9–13; Lk 11:2–4).

■ It is a prayer that God will fulfil his purposes in the world as they are already fulfilled in heaven, together with a request for provisions necessary for today. It offers an intimate and personal relationship with God, referring to God as 'Our Father...'. It is the most famous of all prayers in the Christian Church.

Lord's Supper (C): refers to the last meal which Jesus had with his disciples before his trial and crucifixion.

■ There is some dispute as to whether or not it was a *Passover* meal, but it was certainly a kind of fellowship meal, in which Jesus invited his disciples to eat the bread (representing his body) and drink the wine (representing his blood) as a symbol of the new *covenant* (Lk 22:7–21). This meal forms the basis of the Christian service of Holy *Communion/Mass*.

Luke (NT): probably a Greek physician — friend and companion of Paul who probably travelled with him on some of his journeys and was able to write first-hand accounts of them.

■ He is reputed to be the author of the Gospel of Luke and of the *Acts of the Apostles*.

Luther, Martin (1483–1546) (C): founder of the German *Reformation*.

■ As a lecturer at the University of Wittenberg, he experienced a 'revelation' from God (the 'Tower Experience'), which convinced him that he could receive salvation through his faith alone, without the need for good works. He opposed the sale of indulgences in the Catholic Church and drew up his famous '95 Theses Against Indulgences', pinning them on the door of the church at Wittenberg. This brought him into conflict with the Catholic authorities, and he fled Wittenberg and stayed under the protection of Frederick III of Saxony. In 1519 he denied the primacy of the Pope and in 1520 published three works which challenged the Catholic Church. In 1521 he was excommunicated. However, his ideas had taken hold amongst the people, and unrest had broken out. In 1522 he returned to Wittenberg to restore order. He abolished many Catholic practices and his ideas spread outside Germany. Luther married in 1525. In his later years his work was affected by differences with other Reformers, such as *Zwingli*, and increasing dissensions among his adherents.

Lutheranism (C): movement that follows the teachings of Martin *Luther*, which were expressed in his work ***Catechisms*** (1529) and collected together after his death in the ***Book of Concord*** (1580).

■ Lutheranism upholds the view that scripture is the only rule of faith and all creeds and traditional statements of belief are subordinate to scripture. The principal Lutheran belief is in justification by faith alone. In the years following Luther's death, many of these views were elaborated in an intellectual or scholastic mould which caused much concern; the movement called pietism was a reaction against this intellectualism, calling for a more practical approach to religion. Lutheranism underwent a revival in the twentieth century, and today there are many Lutheran churches around the world.

Magnificat (NT): title given to the song which Mary sings in Luke 1:46–55 to express her joy at being chosen to be the mother of Jesus.

■ It has also been used as a canticle of Vespers in the Western Church, and is included in Evensong in the *Book of Common Prayer* (1549).

Mahabharata (H): 'The Great Epic of the Bharatas' — a compilation of ancient material dating from the second century BCE to the first century CE.

■ The story is set on the upper Ganges plain and deals with the battle between the Kauravas and the Pandavas, who were rival peoples. It reveals much about the ethical values of Hindu society and, in particular, the duties of the individual. The most famous part is the conversation between Krishna, the *avatar* of *Vishnu*, and the hero, Arjuna, which is known as the *Bhagavad Gita* ('Song of the Blessed One').

Mahayana (from Sanskrit, meaning 'great vehicle') **(B):** type of Buddhism common in north Asia (China, Korea, Japan and Tibet), the goal of which is complete Buddhahood through the perfection of wisdom ('*prajna*') and compassion ('karuna').

■ The Mahayana sutras (sayings) date from the second century BCE and show the Buddha as infinitely compassionate, and, through this compassion, he is able to help others. To achieve Buddhahood out of compassion for others is believed in the Mahayana tradition to be greatly superior to achieving personal freedom from one's own suffering and rebirth.

■ *TIP* Mahayana contrasts with *Theravada*, the other main type of Buddhism, in that it emphasises the importance of attaining Buddhahood and holds in high esteem those who have made the vow to attain Buddhahood, the *Bodhisattvas*.

Mahdi (I): Islamic title (meaning 'divinely guided one'), given in *Sunni* Islam to those leaders who come, periodically, to revive the faith when it has grown weak.

■ In particular, towards the last day, a Mahdi, sometimes identified with the returning Jesus, will establish a reign of justice on earth. In *Shi'ah* Islam, the Mahdi is identified with the 'Hidden *Imam*', who will one day reappear and usher in God's rule.

Maimonides, Moses (1135–1204) (J): greatest of the medieval Jewish theologians.

He is most famous for two works: the *Mishnah*, which codifies all rabbinic law and ritual, and 'The Guide for the Perplexed', which highlights Jewish and Aristotelian thought.

Maitreya (B): the *Bodhisattva* accepted by all Buddhist traditions as the next Buddha to come into this world.

 Buddhists believe that there have been many Buddhas in the past and that more will come in the future. Maitreya is said presently to be dwelling in Tushita heaven, awaiting the right time to appear.

Mala'ika (I): in Islam, angels — sometimes described as being made of light — deemed to be superior to humans in general, but inferior to the prophets.

 Certain angels are mentioned specifically in the Qur'an. For instance, Libril (Gabriel) gives the revelation to Muhammad, whilst Iblis is named as the rebel against God and tempter to evil. Other angels mentioned include the angel of death, the keepers of heaven and hell, and the two recording and guardian angels who watch over individual humans.

Mara (meaning 'bringer of death') **(B):** in Buddhist mythology, the tempter — seen as the hold which the world has on the human mind, with the power to seduce and delude it.

 The story of the Buddha's enlightenment is seen as the defeat of Mara.

Maritain, Jacques (1882–1973) (P/E): French philosopher who, in his book *Approaches to God* (1953), attempted to modernise the ideas of St Thomas *Aquinas* — in particular, his 'Five Ways' of proving the existence of God.

 Maritain argued that sense-experience, conceptual thought and scientific method are not the only ways of gaining knowledge. He advocated 'knowledge by inclination', that is, by becoming intuitively aware of tendencies within ourselves which show our true nature, we gain access to the basis for moral knowledge.

Mary, Blessed Virgin (NT/C): mother of Jesus Christ, who appears in the infancy narratives in Luke's Gospel (Lk 1–2), at the wedding in Cana (Jn 2:1–11) and at the Crucifixion (Jn 19:25).

 Mary was given the title 'Mother of God' (*Theotokos*) by the Council of Ephesus in 431 CE and holds a unique place in Roman Catholicism. Special doctrines about her include the notion of her perpetual virginity and the fact that her body was taken up into heaven (the 'Assumption'). Mary is seen to act as a 'Co-Redemptress' with Christ — that is, many believers feel that prayers and devotions made in her honour will be effective in her intercession on their behalf with Christ. Her role is less prominent, but nevertheless important, in the Protestant Church.

Mass (from the Latin *missa*, meaning 'dismissal') **(C):** term used in Roman Catholicism for the *Eucharist*, or Holy Communion in the Protestant tradition.

Mendelssohn, Moses (1729–86) (J): one of the most important Jewish thinkers of the *Enlightenment*.

 He translated the Bible into German and spoke out in favour of educational reforms and religious tolerance towards Jews in his most famous work, *Jerusalem* (1783).

Mennonites (C): followers of Menno Simons (1496–1561), a priest in Dutch Friesland who renounced Roman Catholicism and joined the *Anabaptists*.

■ Menno Simons advocated the baptism of believers and a style of Church organisation that emphasised the responsibility of the congregation. Mennonites became influential in Holland in the seventeenth and eighteenth centuries.

Messiah (from the Hebrew word *mashiach*, meaning 'anointed one') **(OT/NT/J):** said to be the chosen one of God, who will appear at some future time to begin the 'messianic age'.

■ In the Old Testament, the word was sometimes used for someone who had been 'set apart' for a special function, such as a king, who was said to be anointed by God himself. From this came the idea that the future Messiah would come from the line of King David (Matt. 2:1–17).

In the New Testament, the term 'Messiah' is replaced by the Greek word *Christos* (Christ), and is used to refer to Jesus himself. Throughout the Gospels, the messiahship of Jesus is referred to — at his birth (Lk 2:11), by demoniacs (Lk 4:34) and by Peter (Mk 8:29). At his trial, Jesus confesses to being the Christ (Mk 14:61–62).

In Judaism, the Messiah will usher in the new age — the dead will be resurrected, Jewish exiles will return to the Holy Land and humanity will be judged.

■ *TIP* It is very important to be aware that whilst Jesus Christ is seen as the Messiah by Christians, he is not regarded as such by Jews, who still await God's Messiah.

Messianic Secret (NT): theory first put forward by William Wrede in 1901 that Jesus tried to keep the fact that he was the *Messiah* a secret.

■ Wrede observed that in the Gospels Jesus sometimes performed miracles, but then ordered those around him to keep them secret (Mk 5:43; 7:36) — something they often found impossible to do. Similarly, Jesus seemed to tell the *parables* in deliberately obscure language, which apparently concealed some of the truth. However, Wrede's views have been criticised because there are many other instances where Jesus does not attempt secrecy — for example, the triumphal entry into Jerusalem (Lk 19:37–38).

meta-ethics (E): philosophical study of moral judgements and concepts.

■ It seeks the meaning of terms like 'good', 'right' and 'ought', as well as looking at such questions as whether or not there are any such things as moral facts or knowledge.

mezuzah (J): parchment roll on which the first two paragraphs of the Jewish prayer known as the *Shema* are handwritten.

■ A mezuzah is attached to every doorpost in the traditional Jewish home, usually in a decorated case. This is done to fulfil the commandment from Deuteronomy 6:9. Orthodox Jews may kiss the mezuzah on entering or leaving.

Midrash (J): Jewish tradition of biblical interpretation (exegesis) which is found in rabbinical literature.

It attempts to discover the relationship between a biblical idea or theme and the cultural or social context of rabbinical Judaism. In particular, one of the main tasks of Midrash is to reconcile texts which appear to contradict each other.

mikveh (J): pool of natural water used for ritual purification in Judaism, usually constructed by allowing rain-water to collect in a special container.

Converts to Judaism must immerse themselves ('tevilah') in a mikveh, and vessels bought from *Gentiles* must be dipped in one before they can be used to prepare food.

Mill, John Stuart (1806–73) (P/E): London-born philosopher, associated with the ethical theory of *utilitarianism*.

In his work *Utilitarianism* (1861), he argued that people should try to maximise the welfare of everyone and that this welfare meant happiness. He argued for the pursuit of happiness, but said that such happiness should be assessed by quality rather than quantity, and that some forms of happiness are 'higher' than others. In particular, he suggested that pleasures of the mind are more worthy than pleasures of the body.

TIP A very important aspect of ethics. Mill is important because he argues that utilitarianism is not necessarily about 'the greatest happiness for the greatest number' and that certain 'lower' pleasures do not justify the suffering of others. For example, the 'low' pleasure that a group of muggers may get from robbing soneone does not outweigh the pain the victim undergoes.

Millenary Petition (C): petition presented to King James I in 1603 by the *Puritans*, in which they asked to be relieved of their 'common burden of human rites and ceremonies'.

It was followed by the Hampton Court Conference of 1604, between English bishops and the Puritans, and led to slight changes in the *Book of Common Prayer*.

miracle (from the Latin *mirari*, meaning 'to wonder') **(OT/NT/P):** an event or action that goes against the laws of nature and is done through the deliberate action of God.

The classic definition of 'miracle' is stated in David *Hume*'s *An Enquiry Concerning Human Understanding* (1740): '… a transgression of a law of nature by a particular volition of the Deity'.

The writers of the Old Testament believed that God, as the creator of the universe, could and did intervene in the course of nature during vital moments of history — for example, the parting of the Red Sea to allow Moses and the Israelites to escape from the Egyptians (Exod. 14:15–28). Similarly, miraculous healings and other events were prompted by the prayers of the prophets, e.g. 1 Kings 17:17–24.

In the New Testament, the miracles of Jesus and the apostles were seen as signs of God's power and the existence of the *kingdom of God*.

Mishnah (J): rabbinic law which was collected and organised around 200 CE by Rabbi Judah the Prince.

■ The Mishnah is the culmination of the oral tradition, which had been carried out for centuries in Palestine. It covers religious, social and economic matters and comprises 63 tractates.

mitzvah (plural 'mitzvot') **(J):** literally a commandment and, according to tradition, there are 613 mitzvot in the Bible — 248 positive commands and 365 negative ones.

■ The best-known mitzvot are the *Ten Commandments* in Exodus 20:2–17.

moksha (meaning 'liberation') **(B/H):** refers to the goal of the spiritual life of Hindus and Buddhists. It leads to an end of the cycle of death and rebirth.

■ *TIP* 'Moksha' is the term favoured by Hindus; Buddhists tend to use *'nibbana'*.

monasticism (C): system of religious communities, especially monks, living in seclusion from secular society and dedicating their lives to God.

■ The origins of monasticism are unknown, but St Anthony the Great is generally regarded as the first monk. The word 'monk' comes from the Greek *monachos*, meaning 'solitary'. The earliest monks and nuns were people who had abandoned city life and the ethos of the Church (which had become an institution of the Roman Empire) and lived in the desert, seeking God through prayer, fasting and manual labour. They lived in poverty and simplicity in small organisations.
Western monasticism has a distinctive form, which was established following the rules of St Benedict of Nursea. These emphasised a life of discipline and order under the authority of an abbot, who leads the community as a spiritual father.

monotheism (C/I/J): belief that there is one God, most commonly used to describe the supreme, personal creator-God of Christianity and Islam.

moral (from the Latin word *moralis*, meaning 'custom') **(E):** term used to refer to what is regarded as good and bad, right and wrong in human character and behaviour.

■ A moral action, therefore, is one that can be judged according to its good, bad, right or wrong aspects, rather than just its physical quality. 'Moral law' is a law that states which kind of conduct is morally correct, and the term is used by *Kant* in his supreme rule of morality, which he called the *'categorical imperative'*.

moral argument (P): refers to a particular argument for the existence of God that is based on assumptions about morality.

■ The moral argument attempts to show that God exists by using the following assumptions: (1) our moral conscience is, in some sense, the voice of God; (2) moral concepts such as duty and justice would make no sense unless defined in terms of God's will; (3) morality derives its force from rewards and punishments in the future, judged by God; (4) the perfect moral state (*summum bonum*) cannot be achieved in one lifetime — therefore there must be a God who can help us to achieve this state after death.

Moses (OT/NT/J): leader of the Israelites during the time of the *Exodus*.

■ His story begins in Exodus 2:1–10 when, as a baby, he is hidden to escape being killed. He is then brought up in the Egyptian court. As an adult, he encounters God at the Burning Bush (Exod. 3:1–22) and, following a series of devastating plagues sent by God, leads his people out of slavery in Egypt. Under Moses' leadership, the Israelites wander for 40 years in the wilderness, during which time he acts as God's prophet and intercessor. Moses receives the *Ten Commandments* from God (Exod. 20:2–17) and gives the people a sense of national identity. He dies on Mount Nebo, within sight of the Promised Land. In the New Testament, he appears to Jesus at the *Transfiguration* (Lk 9:28–36). In Judaism, Moses is often seen as the greatest of the prophets and is the central figure for rabbinical Judaism.

mosque (from the Arabic word 'masjid', meaning 'place of prostration') **(I):** building in which Muslims meet to worship together, also used for educational and teaching purposes.

The daily worship (*'salat'*) of Islam holds great merit if performed in the mosque, since it is an expression of solidarity with other believers. It is performed on a Friday morning, and a sermon is usually preached. Worship in the mosque requires worshippers to be in a state of ritual purity (*'tahara'*), and fountains are usually provided for this purpose. During worship, believers face towards Mecca in rows, under the leadership of the prayer-leader or *Imam*. In larger mosques there is a slender tower called a minaret, which the muezzin (official who gives the call to prayer) climbs. He calls out from the top of the tower.

Muhammad (I): prophet of Islam.

He was probably born in Mecca c. 570 CE and spent his early life as a merchant. Later, he became convinced that he had been chosen by God (*'Allah'*) to bring God's message to the Arabs. From 610 CE until his death in 632 CE, he received divine revelations, which form the Qur'an. Due to the hostility of the people of Mecca, in 622 CE Muhammad and his followers went to the town of Medina — a move known as the 'hijra', which marks the beginning of the Muslim era. At Medina, Muhammad organised his followers into a powerful group which later went on to capture Mecca and the Arab world. Muhammad is seen as the prophet for all humanity, and his message is said to supersede all previous messages.

Muratorian Canon (NT/C): list written in Latin of the books of the New Testament, dating from the latter half of the second century CE.

The manuscript was discovered by Lodovico Muratori in 1740, and is said to be the oldest known list of writings accepted by the Church as normative.

mysticism (P): refers to those experiences or meditations which lead to an increased awareness and appreciation of God.

myth (P): story that describes other-worldly matters in terms of this world and is a method of interpreting ultimate truths.

Various philosophers have suggested that some of the biblical stories are not literally true but are, in fact, myths — for example, the story of Adam and Eve.

nabi (I): Islamic word for 'prophet', someone sent by God with a message for his people.

■ Before Muhammad, there are said to have been 100,000 prophets, and the Qur'an mentions several who also appear in the Bible, such as Abraham and Jesus. However, Muhammad is seen to be the culmination of the line, and all the scriptures which the 'former' prophets brought are believed to confirm the final revelation of God, the Qur'an.

Nagarjuna (B): said to be a Buddhist thinker who lived for 600 years and performed many miracles. He established the Madhyamaka school of philosophy, discovered the Prajnaparamita scriptures and attained the highest level of *Bodhisattva* practice.

■ Modern scholarship suggests that there may have actually been two Nagarjunas — the first being a second-century Madhyamaka philosopher, and the second an eighth-century alchemist and yogi.

Nam (S): 'divine name', the name of God, and fundamental concept in Sikhism.

■ 'Nam' is an expression for the nature of God, and anything which may be attested to God is an aspect of Nam. 'Nam simaran' is a meditation technique that involves repeating the divine name over and over. The essence of Nam leads to harmony and will enable the meditator to enter into *ineffable* bliss.

natural law (E): theory that everything is created to a particular design and for a particular purpose, and that fulfilling that purpose is the 'good' to which everything aims.

natural theology (C): view that we can understand the nature and existence of God, freedom and immortality through an examination and reflection of the world, taking human existence and thought into account.

■ Natural theology contrasts with *revelation*, which holds that our understanding of God can only come by God revealing himself to us.

near-death experience (P): term often used to describe the experiences which some people believe they have had before being resuscitated from apparent death.

■ The experiences include a feeling of leaving one's body and looking down on the resuscitation process, going on to meet deceased friends and family, travelling down a tunnel to a point of light, and encountering a mystical or religious being. This pattern runs across all religious traditions and is reported by about 35% of all resuscitated persons. Some researchers suggest that this is a product of the brain, such as cerebral anoxia or psychological stress. Others have suggested that it may be consciousness preparing for death.

neo-orthodoxy (C): school of thought in Protestantism which seeks to promote the classical Protestant orthodoxy of the *Reformation* and follows the work of Karl *Barth* (1886–1968).

▨ Neo-orthodoxy holds that theology is about proclaiming the saving power of God through Christ's revelatory activity. It holds that humanity can only know God through divine revelation — mainly through the 'Word of God' manifest in Christ and made known through the Bible.

New Testament (C): second part of the Christian Bible, which forms the basis of the Christian faith.

▨ It comprises 27 books, including the four Gospels and the letters of St Paul.

nibbana (nirvana) (from Sanskrit, meaning 'extinction') **(B/H):** state of highest possible happiness in Buddhism and Hinduism — release from the cycle of reincarnation, extinction of all desires.

▨ Nibbana refers to a state of great inner freedom, in which the mind has supreme tranquillity, purity and stability. It is the goal of all Buddhist saints and their followers.

▨ *TIP* Be careful — do not try to compare nibbana with concepts such as 'heaven' in Christianity. Nibbana is not a 'place' to go when you die; it is a state of being.

Nietzsche, Friedrich (1844–1900) (P): German philosopher, best known as a radical critic of Western traditional beliefs concerning God, truth and morality.

▨ In *Thus Spoke Zarathustra* (1885), Nietzsche said that humankind should become greater and evolve into what he called *Übermensch* ('superman'), a superior type of human being who rejects existing morality by affirming the positive values of earthly life and of the active individual. However, in order to achieve this, those values which derive from Christianity must be abolished first. He believed that the Christian emphasis on the weak, the humble and the virtues of pity and humility, at the expense of the strong, holds humanity back from developing further. His most famous claim was that 'God is dead'.

nihilism (from the Latin *nihil*, meaning 'nothing') **(P):** term used to describe a denial, accompanied by a sense of loss or despair.

▨ It is most commonly used to deny the existence of God, immortality of the soul, freedom, reason, or, in a sense, a 'happy ending' to human history. Applied to individuals, it refers to one who rejects morality or who does not really care about anything.

▨ *TIP* Often used in examinations with reference to the views of *Nietzsche*.

Noah (OT): in the Book of Genesis, a righteous man who is told by God to build an *Ark*, which saves him, along with his family and a wide range of animals, from the great flood.

After the deluge is over, Noah offers a sacrifice and makes a *covenant* with God with laws which are to apply to the whole human race. The promise that there will never again be such a catastrophe is confirmed by the sign of the rainbow. His story is told in Genesis 6–9.

non-cognitivism (P): theory that there is nothing to be known and so there can be no knowledge in the area under consideration. In philosophical terms, it may be used to refer to statements that cannot be proved to be either true or false.

Acclamations ('Praise God!') and ethical statements ('Keep the Sabbath day holy') are examples of non-cognitive statements.

nonconformity (C): refusal to follow the doctrines or disciplines of the Established Church (Church that is officially recognised as a national institution).

It is a term generally used to refer to dissenters from the Church of England.

Nonjurors (C): members of the Church of England who, after 1688, planned to avoid taking the Oaths of Allegiance and Supremacy to William and Mary on the grounds that by doing so they would break their earlier oaths to James II.

The Nonjurors included prominent laypeople, nine bishops and about 400 priests who were denied their livings. This caused a rift within the Church which lasted for many years. By the end of the eighteenth century, however, most of the Nonjurors had been absorbed back into the Established Church.

Numinous (C/P): term first used by Rudolf Otto to explain an experience of the 'holy' — including feelings of awe, religious awareness, the smallness of self and fascination. It is an experience of a spiritual, supernatural or divine character.

Nunc Dimittis (NT): refers to the first words in Latin of the song based on Simeon's words in Luke 2:28–32. Simeon was described as a righteous man to whom it had been revealed by the *Holy Spirit* that he would not die until he had seen the Christ. He meets *Mary* and Joseph at the *Temple* when Jesus is a baby, takes the Christ-child in his arms and says the Nunc Dimittis, which is a canticle of praise for having seen the promise of God's deliverance of his people and the *salvation* of the *Gentiles*.

The song is incorporated today into the evening service in some Churches.

obligation (E): a feeling of being compelled to do a particular action.

▧ In ethics, there are a number of different views on the nature of obligations. One view is that to be under an obligation is to be liable to a punishment if you fail to carry it out — in many primitive cultures, this often meant being under some sort of supernatural 'curse' if you failed to act properly. Another view is that an obligation puts you under the will of another person (or God), who has the authority or right to impose the penalty upon you if you fail to act — this may be authority based not on physical strength, but on a moral aspect. A third view was identified by *Kant*: an obligation to act in a particular way due to reason — the requirements of reason compel you to act in a particular way.

Olam Ha-Ba (J): term in Judaism referring to the hereafter or the 'World to come'.

▧ Originally, it meant the time when the *Messiah* would come (the 'Messianic Age'), but it has also come to refer to the condition of the soul in the afterlife. In the *Talmud* it states that in Olam Ha-Ba there is 'no eating, no drinking, no procreation, no business dealings, no hate and no competition. But the righteous sit with crowns on their heads, deriving pleasure from the radiance of the Divine Presence.'

Old Testament (C/J): first part of the Christian Bible, comprising 39 books which include the *Pentateuch*, the Psalms and the Prophets.

▧ In Judaism, this is called the Hebrew or Jewish Bible.

omnipotent (P): when referring to God, term meaning 'all-powerful'.

omniscient (P): when referring to God, term meaning 'all-knowing'.

ontological argument (P): argument for the existence of God first proposed by *Anselm of Canterbury* in his **Proslogion**.

▧ It makes three points: (1) God is a being greater than which none can be conceived; (2) such a being exists either in the imagination or in reality; (3) a being that exists in reality is greater than one which exists only in the imagination — therefore the greatest conceivable being exists in reality. The French philosopher René Descartes (1596–1650) took this a stage further, by suggesting that: (1) God is a being with every positive perfection, and therefore he lacks nothing; (2) a being which does not exist in reality lacks something. Therefore God exists in reality.

O

■ *TIP* A very important aspect of philosophy of religion. Questions usually ask for contrast with the *teleological* and *cosmological arguments*. Ensure that you understand both the strengths and the weaknesses of the ontological argument before answering any questions on it.

original sin (NT/C): in Christian theology, doctrine of the sin of Adam (the '*Fall of Man*'), which has affected all humanity ever since — human sin, therefore, can be traced back to Adam's 'original sin'.

■ The doctrine is highlighted in Romans 5:12 — 'Therefore, sin entered the world through one man [Adam]...'

orthodox (C): term referring to those beliefs that are accepted by a religious system as being 'right' belief, as opposed to wrong belief, or heresy.

■ In Christianity, the beliefs were ratified by the early Church as being in accordance with God's revelation in scripture and in the experience of the earliest Christian believers.

Oxford Movement (C): movement in the Church of England that tried to restore High Church principles.

■ It started in the early nineteenth century — specifically in 1833, with John Keble's sermon at Oxford. Some clergymen were concerned at what they saw as a decline in standards and a trend towards *liberalism* within the Church. The aims of the movement were threefold: firstly, to defend the Church of England as a divine institution; secondly, to uphold the doctrine of Apostolic Succession, which was the method whereby the ministry of the Church was seen to be derived directly from the original Apostles of Jesus by a continuous succession of bishops; and thirdly, to defend the position of the ***Book of Common Prayer*** as a rule of faith.

Paccekabuddha (B): Buddhist term for an 'individual' Buddha who becomes enlightened by discovering the eternal truth of the way things are by themselves.

■ This is in contrast to the *Arahat*, who becomes enlightened by following teachings of a fully awakened Buddha. Paccekabuddha is an important concept in *Theravada* Buddhism.

Paley, William (1743–1805) (E): clergyman who wrote *Principles of Moral and Political Authority* (1785), in which he formulated a kind of theological *utilitarianism* based on the notion that the basis of moral duty was to obey God's commands.

■ He argued that God's commands are known to us, both through the Bible and from natural reason. God wills the greatest possible happiness for all, and so it is our duty to follow God's will in order to maximise happiness.

Pali (from Sanskrit, meaning 'scriptural text') **(B):** language of the *Theravada* Buddhist scriptures.

■ It was originally called 'Magadha' and was said to have been the language spoken by the Buddha.

panentheism (P): doctrine that all things are in God. It stems from the words of Acts 17:28 — 'For in him we live and move and have our being.'

■ The term was first used by C. F. Krause in 1828 and adopted by A. N. Whitehead (1861–1947) in his work on process theodicy.

pantheism (P): notion that the world as a whole, and nature in its widest sense, are identified with God.

■ In a sense, reality is divine and God and nature are equated. Sense-experience is said to be an illusion, and only the divine is real.

■ *TIP* Panentheism and pantheism are not the same — in the latter the world is identified with God, in the former it is not, although the world remains dependent on God.

parables (C): stories, similes or metaphors that use real-life examples to illustrate a religious or moral/ethical truth.

■ Although most famously used by Jesus, parables were widely used by Jewish teachers.

Paraclete (Greek for 'one called to the side of', 'advocate') **(NT):** term for the Holy Spirit mainly used in John's Gospel (e.g. Jn 16:5–16).

■ The role of advocate suggests that the Spirit will act as the defence for the Apostles in times of trouble (Jn 14:15–31).

paradox (P): an impossible truth.

■ In Christianity, it may be used to refer to such doctrines as the *Trinity* — one God in Three Persons.

parousia (from the Greek for 'presence') **(NT):** term used in the New Testament to refer to the *Second Coming* of Christ, which is his final return at the end of time, e.g. 1 Corinthians 15:23.

■ It refers to a time of the judgement of the living and the dead, and the end of the present world order.

■ *TIP* Many in the early Church believed that the Second Coming of Christ was imminent, and this can be an important aspect of discussion in New Testament/early Church history examinations.

Parvati (H): Hindu goddess and wife of *Shiva* — her name means 'daughter of the mountain'.

■ In art and literature, Shiva and Parvati are seen as deeply in love, although quarrelsome. Their children are Ganesha and Karttikeya. Parvati appears in many forms; in Shiva's presence she is gentle and royal, holding a lotus, but away from him she can be the formidable *Durga* or *Kali*.

Pascal's wager theory (P): theory devised by Blaise Pascal (1623–62) in which he suggests humans should settle any doubt they have regarding whether or not God exists by framing it in terms of a bet, or wager.

■ Pascal claimed that, if God exists, then he is unknowable and so humans are unable to use their powers of reason to determine whether or not he exists. Instead, we must make up our minds with a bet: if we bet that he does exist and so lead a godly life, then we 'win' an eternity of bliss; if we gamble that he does not exist and lose, then we could lose our eternal life.

Passover (*Pesach* in Hebrew) **(J):** Jewish festival that commemorates the freeing of the Israelites from slavery in Egypt (Exod. 12:31–42).

■ It is an annual festival, held on the fourteenth day of the month of Nisan. In biblical times, the festival would revolve around the sacrifice of a Pascal lamb, which would then be eaten. Today, a ritual family meal is held on the first night of Passover (the 'sedar' night), in which the Exodus story is retold and the youngest child asks four questions ('mah nishtanah') about the meal and four cups of wine are drunk, symbolising the divine help and redemption of God. Bitter herbs are eaten to symbolise suffering, and *unleavened bread* symbolises the diet of the slaves.

■ *TIP* The Passover meal is regarded in the Synoptic Gospels (Mathew, Mark and Luke) as the meal Jesus ate with his disciples before his death ('the Last Supper'). Jesus is also sometimes identified with the sacrificial lamb, e.g. 1 Corinthians 5:7. Both of these points may be important in New Testament examinations.

Patimokkha (B): code of the Buddhist monastery, to which all fully ordained members must adhere.

▨ The rules are divided into categories and there are four fundamental prohibitions — against sexual intercourse, theft, intentional killing of a human being or deception of laypeople. Failure to abide by any of these means 'defeat', and the individual is permanently barred from the monastery.

Patriarch (OT): principal ancestor or father-figure of the Israelites. The Patriarchs were Abraham, Isaac and Jacob.

▨ God promised Abraham that he would make him into a great nation (Gen. 12:2) and that he would have as many children as there are stars in the sky (Gen. 15:5). This made him the first Patriarch, and the promise continues through the offspring of his son Isaac and grandson Jacob — from their children come the twelve *tribes of Israel*.

Paul (c. 6 BCE–64 CE) (NT): Jew and Roman citizen, one of the first Christian missionaries to the *Gentiles*.

▨ Paul was persecuting members of the early Church when he was temporarily blinded by God in a vision of the risen Jesus. After recovering his sight, he changed his name from Saul to Paul and he became a member of the early Church. He spent much of his life travelling in the Roman world spreading the Gospel of Christ and helping to set up new churches in the Gentile world. His missionary journeys are recorded in the book of the *Acts of the Apostles*. He was executed in Rome by the Emperor Nero.

Paul's letters to the early churches and communities are recorded in the New Testament, and they contain much detailed teaching on worship, *spiritual gifts*, election, *resurrection*, and *salvation* and *redemption* through Christ.

penance (C): Christian *sacrament* for the forgiveness of sins.

▨ It usually requires the penitent person to make a private confession to a priest, who will then formally pronounce the person forgiven and order certain 'penances' (penalties or punishments) to be undertaken.

Pentateuch (OT/J): name given to the first five books of the Bible — known in Judaism as 'the law of Moses' or the *'Torah'*.

▨ For Jews, the Pentateuch is the holiest part of the Bible.

Pentecost (NT/J): Jewish festival (called 'Shavuot' in Hebrew) that occurs 50 days after *Passover* — a period known as the 'omer', or 'counting' (or sometimes 'the Feast of Weeks').

▨ It is a festival which celebrates the wheat harvest and commemorates the giving of the *Ten Commandments* to Moses (seen as 'bread from heaven'). Synagogues are decorated with flowers at this time, in honour of the harvest, and many Jews stay awake the night before to study the Torah. In the morning service, the Book of Ruth is read, which is set at harvest time.

In the New Testament, Pentecost is remembered as the time when the *Holy Spirit* came down to the *Apostles* in tongues of fire (Acts 2:1–4).

Peter (NT): one of Jesus' disciples, traditionally seen as their leader. He was originally called Simon, but Jesus changed his name to Peter (Greek for 'rock' — see John 1:42).

▨ Peter was originally a fisherman but became the most prominent of all the disciples. He came nearer than any of the others to recognising Jesus' messiahship (Mk 8:29). He is present at the *Transfiguration* (Mk 9:2–13; Lk 9:28–36) and, during the time of Jesus' arrest and trial, denies three times that he even knows him (Lk 22:54–62; Jn 18:15–18, 25–27). After the *Resurrection*, he meets the risen Jesus and is given the commission to carry on the work of Christ (Jn 21:15–19). He becomes a prominent leader in the early Church (Acts 2:14–41), is put on trial before the Jewish leaders (Acts 4:1–22) and plays a major role in the admission of *Gentiles* to the Church (Acts 10:1–48; 15:7–11). He was executed, probably by crucifixion in Rome, around 64 CE.

In the Roman Catholic tradition, Peter is said to have been the first Bishop of Rome.

Pharisees (from Aramaic, meaning 'separated ones') **(NT):** strict religious group within Judaism that figures prominently in the life of Jesus, who frequently argues with them.

▨ They were mostly ordinary Jews who stuck closely to the Jewish Law and lived very strict lives. They extended the Law to cover every detail and were sometimes accused of losing sight of the spirit behind it. Jesus condemns their self-righteousness and legalism in Luke 5:21–23, 6:1–11 and John 9:1–41. The most famous Pharisees were Nicodemus (Jn 3:1–21) and Paul.

Philistines (OT): sea-going people who settled along the coast in the south of Palestine and became enemies with the Israelites, with whom they had a long-running conflict that was ended by King David's victory over them (2 Sam. 8:1).

▨ They lived in five main cities: Gaza, Ashdod, Ashkelon, Gath and Ekron. The most famous Philistine was Goliath (1 Sam. 17:1–58).

pietism (C): movement in Lutheranism led by Spener (1635–1705) and Francke (1663–1705) which highlighted the need for practical and inward religion, rather than dogmatic attitudes.

▨ The aim of the movement was to bring new vigour to the Church by restoring prayer circles and Bible reading, and proclaiming that all believers had a special relationship with God.

Pillars of Islam (I): basic institutions of the Islamic law which are required of every adult male believer.

▨ The five pillars are: the profession of faith ('*shahada*'), worship ('*salat*'), alms giving ('*zakat*'), pilgrimage ('*hajj*') and fasting ('suam'). To these is sometimes added a sixth, namely holy warfare ('*jihad*').

Plato (427–347 BCE) (E/P): Greek philosopher and founder of the Academy in Athens. His writings are mostly in the form of 'dialogues', with Socrates as the main speaker.

▨ In his early Dialogues the emphasis is on ethics. Plato believed that the most important thing was to cultivate the will and the mind — what he called the

p

'goodness of the soul'. This is achieved by rational insight into the nature of beauty, truth and goodness. A person may become rational and moral through a 'recollection' of what the soul knows about these values. The soul naturally aims at what it perceives to be good. Wrongdoing is the following of falsely conceived good. In the later Dialogues, Plato contrasts the world of sense and everyday experience with what he sees as a true or higher form of ideas or 'Forms', such as justice and holiness. By understanding these Forms and participating in them, the soul achieves wellbeing. The secret of human destiny is found in the soul's search for the good, which it sees, but does not possess. In one of his most famous works, the **Republic**, Plato suggests that the human soul is composed of three parts: reason, spirit and desire. When these are all working perfectly, the individual is morally virtuous and just. Moral failure happens when the parts are not balanced and functioning properly.

Plymouth Brethren (C): Protestant group that began in England, inspired by the work of J. N. Darby (1800–32).

▧ The Plymouth Brethren centre their worship on the *'breaking of bread'*, a simple rite which acts as a memorial to Christ's Last Supper. There are two main types of Brethren: the 'Open' and the 'Exclusives'. The 'Exclusives' have demanding standards and reject many aspects of modern life. They will rarely have contact with non-Brethren.

polytheism (P): belief in, or worship of, many gods.

prajna (B): Buddhist term, broadly translated as 'wisdom', which refers to a mental process associated with insight into the true meaning of things.

▧ It is classed, along with *'sila'* and *'samadhi'*, as the third of the three constituents of the Buddhist path and is regarded as the most important of the six perfections ('paramita') attained by the *Bodhisattva* on the way to Buddhahood. It is generally thought to come from an investigation by the individual into how things really are. Through meditation, the believer gains experience and understanding of the true way of things and, therefore, the ultimate truth.

prayer (C/I/J/H/S): in Christianity, the act of communicating, in words or silence, with God. It rests on the belief that God has a personal nature and that humanity is able to have a relationship with him. Prayer may be of several types — adoration and worship, intercession (praying for the needs of others), penitence (asking for forgiveness) and petition (asking for something). It may be a conversation between the individual and God, or a 'common' prayer, said together by several people in a service of worship. The most famous prayer is the *'Lord's Prayer'*, taught by Jesus to his disciples (Matt. 6:9–13; Lk 11:2–4).

In Islam, prayer is seen as a direct communication with God (*Allah*), and ritual prayers (*salah/salat*) are part of the *Pillars of Islam* that Muslims are required to observe. In times of prayer, worshippers must undergo special washing to make themselves ritually clean ('wudu') — a cleansing of the body and the soul from sin. Ritual prayers are said five times a day, at dawn, noon, mid-afternoon, sunset and night. Muslims may also use private prayer to praise God, to ask for what they need and to seek forgiveness.

In Judaism, prayer is seen as communication with God and the opportunity to judge one's life and conduct. The *Talmud* defines prayer as the 'service of the heart' and an expression of the believer's inner self. Jewish prayer services end with the hope that the *Messiah* will arrive soon. The most famous prayer in Judaism is the *Shema*.

In Hinduism, prayer is part of daily worship (*puja*) and may include offerings to the deities and recitals of prayers such as the 'Gayatri mantra'.

In Sikhism, the most famous formal prayers are the *ardas*, or 'petition', which are said in the morning and evening after reading the scriptures. Prayer includes praising God for the teachings of the *Gurus*, and requests for help and guidance.

predestination (C): notion that God has prearranged plans for certain people.

■ It is associated with the idea that, in some way, God has already decided that some people will be 'saved' and others 'condemned'. It is supported by biblical references in Matthew 20:23, where Jesus says that seats on his right and left in his kingdom will 'belong to those for whom they have been prepared by my Father'. Later, in Romans 8:29, Paul says of God: 'those he predestined, he also called.' In the Christian Church, *Calvin* made predestination the cornerstone of his system, suggesting that Christ's death was for the *atonement* of the elect (or 'predestined') alone. Modern mainstream Christian thought tends to follow the line that humans are free to choose the path they wish to follow, and that it is God's intention, if possible, for all to be saved.

■ *TIP* This is a very controversial subject within the Christian Church, since it may suggest that salvation is not for everyone, which seems, to some, to contradict the teaching of Jesus and the early Church.

priest (OT/NT/C): in the Christian tradition, a priest is seen as a representative of God to his people.

■ In the Old Testament, priests were intermediaries between God and humanity. Their main task was to offer sacrifices. They were also responsible for the sacred lots '*Urim and Thummim*' (Exod. 28:30). During the time of the Judges, priests of the tribe of Levi ('*Levites*') were highly valued, but much of this status was lost when local shrines closed and worship was centralised in Jerusalem. In New Testament times, chief priests, together with elders and scribes, made up the body known as the *Sanhedrin*, in front of which Jesus appeared before being sent for trial by Pilate (Lk 22:66–71; Jn 18:19–24). In the early Church, the whole body of Christians was regarded as a 'royal priesthood' (1 Peter 2:5), whose task was to pray for God's blessing on the world.

In the Christian Church today, the parish priest will normally be the one who leads the *Eucharist* service, and may exercise the power of absolution. Priests are usually ordained and are under the general guidance of the bishop.

probability (P): degree of confidence that a particular occurrence will take place. This may range from 'certain' to 'impossible'.

proof (P): evidence that something is the case.

prophet (OT): someone whom God has chosen and to whom he has communicated a message, usually through a vision or prophetic inspiration. The prophet will then give God's message to the people.

■ In the Old Testament, prophets were generally 'seers' who received visions or messages in dreams or divination. Moses is regarded by many as the greatest of the Old Testament prophets — a man of authority who spoke to God face to face (Num. 12:8) and was able to perform 'wonders' (Deut. 18:15–22). The most commonly held view about the prophets was that they were able to foretell future events. They gave messages from God urging the people to change their ways in order to avoid trouble in the future, e.g. *Amos* and *Hosea*. Prophets sometimes held positions of importance and respect in the religious and social life of the Hebrews — both *Isaiah* and *Jeremiah* received royal protection, whilst *Samuel* was empowered to appoint a king. Other prophets, such as Elijah and Elisha, sometimes performed miracles.

Protestantism (C): system of Christian faith and practice that is based upon an acceptance of the principles of the *Reformation*. The name comes from the protests (***protestatio***) against Roman Catholicism by the reforming members of the Diet of Speyer in 1529.

■ The major groups in original Protestantism were *Lutheranism*, *Calvinism* and *Zwinglianism* and, later, the Church of England. The main tenets of Protestantism are an acceptance of the Bible as the only source of revealed truth, the doctrine of *justification* by faith alone, and the universal priesthood of all believers. It emphasises the transcendence of God, *original sin* and the inability of unaided humanity to gain knowledge of God. Compared to Roman Catholicism, worship is less ceremonial and has fewer sacramental elements, and there is greater emphasis on the preaching of the Word.

providence (P): notion that God foresees and controls future events in order to care for his creation and to enable all things to work for his divine purpose.

puja (H): worship in Hinduism — mainly of three kinds: temple worship, domestic worship and communal worship.

■ The temple is seen as the home of the god, and the god, along with their consort and associated gods, will be represented in the temple — most commonly as statues. The deities are served by priests ('pujari') who carry out a programme of worship at set times of the day, beginning at dawn when the deity is ceremonially woken, accompanied by the sound of bells, the conch and religious music. The worshipper coming to the temple seeks to obtain a *'darshana'* — a sight or experience of the deity — and may also make a special request or petition to the deity relating to everyday matters.

Domestic worship usually centres around a part of the house which has been set aside in a state of ritual purity. The area will normally contain an image of the household's chosen deity, to which prayers are directed and offerings made.

Communal worship may involve hymn singing or a recitation of a religious text by a priest before an audience.

punna (B): in Buddhism, 'punna' refers to those actions an individual performs that are especially worthy and will bring good results and create opportunities to practise the Buddha's teaching.

Such actions may include the making of devotional offerings, giving alms to members of the *Sangha*, taking the precepts, going for refuge (*'tisarana'*) and practising meditation.

Purana (H): one of a series of sacred writings that deal with ancient times and events, probably dating from the fourth century CE onwards.

There are 18 principal Puranas, divided into three types: those which exalt Brahma, those which exalt Vishnu and those which exalt *Shiva*. Unlike the *Vedas*, the Puranas have been available to, and known by, the lower-*caste* people and have not been kept in the hands of the *Brahmans*.

Purgatory (C): in Catholic theology, a state or place where individuals who have died in the grace of God expiate their unforgiven venial sins (serious sins, but not ones which will deprive the soul of God's grace) and undergo punishment for their forgiven sins, if such punishment is due. After this, they are admitted into heaven.

Puritans (C): extreme English Protestants who were dissatisfied with the religious settlement of Elizabeth I and who tried to purify the Church from what they saw as unscriptural forms and corruption.

They were prominent amongst the merchant classes and attacked the use of vestments, ornaments and signs of the Cross. The term 'Puritan' ceased to be used after 1660.

'Q' (initial letter of the German word *Quelle*, meaning 'source') **(NT):** symbol used to refer to material which is common to the Gospels of both Matthew and Luke but not found in Mark, and which consists of about 230 verses, most of which contain the sayings of Jesus.

■ Supporters of what is known as the 'Q' hypothesis, such as B. H. Streeter (1924–), believe that there was once a document ('Q'), now lost, which contained a record of many of the teachings of Jesus. It was used by the writers of both Matthew and Luke, and might explain the similarities in the two Gospels (e.g. Matthew 3:7–10 compared with Luke 3:7–9). The 'Q' hypothesis is only a theory, and some New Testament scholars reject it.

qiyama (I): in Islam, the resurrection that follows the last judgement.

■ Islamic *eschatology* suggests that, at the end of all things, the angel Israfil will physically raise the dead, who will then be judged by God, who will weigh up their good and bad deeds. The judged souls must then pass across a narrow bridge — sinners will fall off into hell, but the saved will enter paradise.

Quest of the Historical Jesus (C): phrase used to describe attempts to determine the actual character of the teaching, faith and events in the life of Jesus.

■ It comes from the title of a book by Albert Schweitzer (1875–1965) in which he traced the course of investigation by scholars into the presentation of Jesus in the Gospels. The 'quest' highlighted the fact that scholars have tended to mould a picture of Jesus according to their own particular convictions and leanings. The 'quest' is continued today by scholars, especially those with an interest in sociology and the social environment in which Jesus lived and worked.

Qumran (NT/C/J): Arabic name for the site of a monastery near the Dead Sea, about 14 km (9 miles) from Jericho, in which a Jewish group known as the *Essenes* were said to have lived from the second century BCE until the Jewish Revolt in 66–70 CE.

■ It was at Qumran that the *Dead Sea Scrolls* were discovered in 1947.

Qur'an (I): sacred book of Islam, said to be the uncreated word of God which existed before the world and was given to the Arabs through the Prophet Muhammad in a series of revelations.

It is regarded as a message for all humanity, and replaces imperfect and corrupted previous versions of heavenly scripture. The message is God's alone and has had no human interference. The text is sacred in itself, and a believer must be in a state of ritual purity (*'tahara'*) before touching a copy. It is divided into 'suras', or chapters, proclaiming the unity of God, giving thanks and offering obedience to God, and outlining legal and social topics which are embodied in the law of Islam.

rabbi (NT/J): (1) form of address, rather like 'sir', at the time of Christ — used slightly differently in the Gospels to refer to Jesus with particular reverence, indicating that he had special authority (Mk 10:51); (2) in later Judaism, general term for an authority or teacher of the oral Torah.

■ In John's Gospel, Jesus is addressed as 'rabbi' by two of his disciples and by Nicodemus, who calls him a rabbi because he can perform 'miraculous signs' (Jn 3:2). At the *Resurrection*, Mary addresses the risen Jesus as 'rabboni' or 'my teacher' (Jn 20:16).

■ *TIP* A rabbi in Judaism is not a priest, but is seen more as a teacher or spiritual guide.

Rama (H): incarnation ('*avatar*') of the Hindu God *Vishnu*.

■ His life is recorded in the epic known as 'Ramayana', in which he defeats the demon Ravana. He is depicted as the ideal man and a role model for human behaviour, while his wife, Sita, is the ideal woman.

In art, Rama is blue in colour and holds a bow and arrow. He is usually accompanied by Sita and *Hanuman*, the monkey-god.

rational argument (P): argument based on reason or empirical evidence (touch, hearing, sight etc.).

rationalism (P): in philosophy, theory developed in the seventeenth century that there are certain kinds of knowledge which can be known through the operation of reason, rather than being based on experience — in contrast to empiricism.

■ It emphasises the authority of human reason, with religious beliefs being seen as expressions of human hopes, and morality as the action of conscience. The main rationalist philosophers were René Descartes (1596–1650), Benedict Spinoza (1632–77) and Gottfried Leibnitz (1646–1716).

redaction criticism (OT/NT/C): one aspect of *biblical criticism* — in this case, the study of how the authors, particularly of the Gospels, shaped the material they used in different ways.

■ For example, the story of Jesus walking on the water in Mark 6:45–52 appears in a different form in Matthew 14:22–33, where Peter attempts to copy Jesus. Redaction criticism here might suggest that the author of Matthew's Gospel was adding themes to do with discipleship. Some of the most influential scholars in this field are Bornkamm, Conzelmann and Marxsen.

redemption (OT/NT/C): biblical notion, stemming from the idea of being delivered or saved from evil by a 'redeemer' who 'pays the price' for our freedom.

In the Old Testament, there were rules governing the 'ransom' that needed to be paid to free someone, e.g. from sentence of death (Exod. 21:30), and God was seen as the one who will 'deliver' or free his people (Is. 41:14). In the New Testament, Christ is seen as the redeemer whose death on the Cross 'pays the price' of human sin and allows for salvation (Gal. 1:3–4; Heb. 2:17). In Christianity, redemption is seen as a free gift from God to sinful humanity, which could not save itself, but is saved through the redeeming death of Christ.

Reformation (C): religious movement in Europe at the end of the Middle Ages — an attempt by reformers such as *Luther, Calvin* and *Zwingli* to emphasise the teaching and authority of the Bible over that of the Pope.

It included such themes as salvation through faith rather than by works, and a simplification of the sacraments and worship. The religious changes of the Reformation were joined by social and political changes which led to a split in the Western Church into Roman Catholicism and Protestantism.

reincarnation (P/B/H): notion that, after the death of the body, the soul moves to another body.

According to Hinduism, the soul was never born and will never die, but undergoes continuous incarnations until it is released into some higher existence.

Buddhists do not believe that the soul is immortal, and see reincarnation as the flow of consciousness between one life and the next.

TIP In philosophy of religion examinations, reincarnation is also referred to as 'rebirth', 'transmigration of the soul' and 'metempsychosis'. Questions often centre on the differences between reincarnation and other concepts, such as the immortality of the soul. A very common theme is the link between the body and the mind, and how this is affected in reincarnation.

remnant (OT/NT): in the Old Testament, term used to refer to the group of Jews who had escaped or who would not be destroyed because it had remained faithful (Amos 5:15).

The prophet *Isaiah* taught that a remnant of the nation would remain, whereas *Jeremiah* suggested that the remnant would suffer much hardship but would, eventually, be saved (Jer. 23:3–4).

In the New Testament, Paul highlighted the fact that a remnant of the Jewish people had turned to Christ (Rom. 11:5).

repentance (OT/NT/C): remorse for one's past action, producing a change of mind or behaviour. It is a radical change and is meant to be a permanent one.

In the Old Testament, repentance is sometimes required of the whole people — meaning that they should turn back to God (Amos 5:4; Hos. 6:1–4), and if so they will be forgiven (Is. 1:18–19).

In the New Testament, John the Baptist calls for repentance prior to the ministry of Jesus, and such repentance could be displayed by the outward sign of baptism (Lk 3:21–22; Jn 1:29–34).

In the Christian Church, there is a requirement for repentance amongst believers, which includes sorrow for sins committed, confession of guilt and forgiveness.

Resurrection (NT/C/I/J): belief found in Judaism, Christianity and Islam that, at the end of time, God will 'reassemble' the dead and restore them to life. In Christianity, the rising again of Christ from the tomb, 3 days after his death.

■ The Resurrection of Christ is one of the central themes of Christianity. After his death on Good Friday, Christ rose to life on Easter Sunday. He is 'resurrected' in the sense of being 'rebuilt' (rather than 'resuscitated', which just means bringing his body back to life), and it is seen as both a physical and a spiritual resurrection to life. According to the Gospels, the risen Jesus has a physical body (Lk 24:30–32; Jn 23–24), but also has 'extra' qualities — he can, apparently, pass into locked rooms. He appears to the disciples on several occasions before finally ascending into heaven (Acts 1:9). For Christians, the Resurrection highlights the triumph of the Cross, of good over evil, love over hate, and of *atonement* and forgiveness of sins (1 Cor. 15:21–22).

revealed theology (P/C): system of theology based on God's revelation to humanity and not based on what humans have deduced for themselves through reason or logic.

revelation (NT): term given to knowledge that is imparted to humanity from God himself, either through visions (Jer. 1:4–19), or as a divine gift or message (Gal. 1:12), or passed to others through an understanding of the events of history (Ps. 111:4).

■ 'Revelation' is also the name given to the final book of the New Testament.

righteousness (OT/NT): (1) in the Old Testament, quality of being right or innocent; (2) in the New Testament, term used in its ethical or religious sense — that is, doing the will of God (Matt. 5:20).

■ In the Old Testament, for example, it is used when talking about a good king (Is. 32:1) or neighbour (Amos 5:7). Above all, God is seen as righteous because he follows the *covenant* and will save his people (Jer. 23:5–6).

In the New Testament, Paul (Rom. 3:21–22) suggests that righteousness includes not only right conduct, but also a right relationship with God.

Roman Catholicism (C): faith and practice of Christians who are in communion with the Pope. This is in contrast to Protestantism.

■ The Roman Catholic Church is the largest Church in Western Christianity and is made up of a hierarchy of priests and bishops, with the Pope at its head. Emphasis is placed upon the importance of the seven *sacraments* and the *Mass*.

Rosh Hashanah (Hebrew for 'head of the year') **(J):** 2-day festival of the Jewish New Year.

■ The year begins in the autumn, and Rosh Hashanah is remembered as a time of judgement when God judges the deeds of humanity over the past year. The festival starts the 10 days of repentance, which culminate in the fast of *Yom Kippur*. Rosh Hashanah is a festive day, celebrated with good food and drink as a sign of the trust of the Jews in God's mercy and forgiveness.

rule utilitarianism (E): method of deciding the 'rightness' of an action. The earliest proponent of the theory was John Austin in his work ***The Province of Jurisprudence*** (1832), and this was followed by John Stuart *Mill* in ***Utilitarianism*** (1861).

■ It is done in stages: (1) one has to find the best rule of conduct in a given situation, and this is done by looking at what the consequences will be of following a particular rule — the rule which has the best consequences is the best rule to follow; (2) the right action is the one which conforms with the best rule. The main problem with rule utilitarianism is that it requires us to consider the consequences of the general following of a particular rule, which may not necessarily produce the right result in one's particular situation. For instance, in most countries the rule is that people drive on the right. In Britain, people drive on the left. According to rule utilitarianism, we should keep to the right — but that would cause an accident in Britain!

Sabbath (OT/NT/C/J): term that comes from the notion of 'cessation from work', referring to the weekly day of rest and devotion to God.

▪ In Judaism, the Sabbath is the seventh day of the week (Saturday), linking with the notion in Genesis chapter 2 that, after creating the world in 6 days, God rested on the seventh. In the Old Testament, the Sabbath was seen as a day of rejoicing and going to the *Temple*, and the *Ten Commandments* required people to 'Remember the Sabbath Day by keeping it holy' (Exod. 20:8–11). Jesus worshipped in the synagogue on the Jewish Sabbath (Lk 4:16) and ran into conflict with the Jewish authorities by allowing his disciples to pick grain (Lk 6:1–11) on the Sabbath and by healing on the Sabbath (Lk 13:10–17). In Christianity, the Sabbath is celebrated on Sunday, the first day of the week, in line with Jesus' resurrection on Easter Sunday.

Sach-khand (S): in Sikhism, condition of bliss which awaits all who have persevered in the practice of 'Nam simaran', meditation on the divine name of God.

▪ Sach-khand is a 'Realm of Truth' where all is peace and disharmony is stilled. Some see it as a kind of heavenly dwelling place.

sacraments (from the Latin *sacramentum*, meaning 'vow') **(C):** outward and visible signs which Christians believe have been ordained by Jesus to symbolise and convey inward and spiritual grace.

▪ In the Protestant tradition, only two sacraments are recognised — *baptism* and the *Eucharist*. However, in the Catholic tradition there are seven recognised sacraments — baptism, confirmation, *Mass*, marriage, *penance*, unction and orders (priestly ordination).

sacrifice (OT/NT): offering of a gift to the deity, sometimes a living creature. In early Christianity it was used mainly as a means of either seeking forgiveness for sin or asking for God's help (e.g. for a plentiful harvest).

▪ Whatever was sacrificed had to be of value, since the one making the sacrifice had to be seen to be losing something of value. If it was not an animal, then the sacrifice might be an offering of the best grain or produce. In biblical times, sacrifices were made to God by Cain and Abel (Gen. 4:3–5), and God demands the sacrifice of *Abraham*'s son, Isaac, in Genesis 22:1–16. Sacrifices were

S

associated with the making of the *covenant* (Exod. 24:5), and elaborate temple rituals were later introduced. The main sacrifice was that of the Paschal Lamb at the *Passover*. In the New Testament, Christ himself is seen as the sacrifice — death and his blood being the signs of the new covenant (Rom. 3:25).

Sadducees (NT): small but powerful group in Judaism during the time of Christ.

■ They were traditionalists in their faith and observed the written law. They opposed armed conflict and did not resist the Roman occupation of Israel, choosing instead to compromise, which made them unpopular with many of the people. They rejected the views of the *Pharisees* on the oral law and did not believe in the immortality of the soul or the resurrection of the body. Jesus came into conflict with them on several occasions (Matt. 16:1–12; Mk 12:18–27). The Sadducees ceased to exist after the destruction of the *Temple* in 70 CE.

sadhu (meaning 'one who is straight') **(H):** in Hinduism, term referring to a worthy and honourable person who has renounced the ordinary life. In Hindu tradition, the sadhu is usually a saint.

saint (C): in Christianity, someone who is faithful to God throughout their lifetime (Ps. 31:23) and is dedicated to God's service (Dan. 7:18).

■ Saints are believers (1 Cor. 6:1) who belong to Jesus and are 'loved by God' (Rom. 1:7). In the Book of Revelation, they are depicted as martyrs for the faith. In the Catholic Church, a holy person, after their death, may go through the process of canonisation, in which their lives are investigated, and they may then be declared to be a saint. Many days are deemed to be saints' days, and devotion to saints is common in the Catholic Church (much less so in the Protestant tradition).

salat/salah (I): in Islam, the sequence of utterances and actions which make up Muslim worship.

■ Salat is one of the five *Pillars of Islam*, and all able-bodied adults are required to perform the salat five times a day.

salvation (C): from the Hebrew notion of 'safety' or 'deliverance', the state whereby a believer is removed from danger into a place of safety and protection.

■ In Christianity, this means that, through God's grace, the believer is freed from sin and reconciled to God. According to Paul, those who have faith will receive salvation and escape from the perils of future judgement by God (Rom. 13:11; 1 Thess. 1:10).

Salvation Army (C): international Christian organisation founded by William Booth in 1865.

■ It is organised on a military basis, and is renowned for its evangelical and social work.

samadhi (B): Buddhist term that roughly translates as 'concentration' — the practice of yoga and meditation.

■ Samadhi is the mind's ability to rest or concentrate on a particular object as part of the meditation process. This leads to the attainment of various states of consciousness in which the mind becomes absorbed with the object being contemplated. These states may lead to higher levels of knowledge.

samantha (B): one of two types of Buddhist meditation practice that seek to bring about a state of inner peace by overcoming the five 'hindrances': greed, anger, sloth, excitement and doubt.

■ The emphasis is on training in alertness and joyful contentment.

Samaritans (NT): people who settled in the area of Samaria (north of Jerusalem) in biblical times.

■ They practised a form of Hebrew worship which was mixed with other cultic influences and, as such, were hated and despised by the Jews in Judea, even though they had much in common with each other. Jesus showed friendliness towards them (Jn 4:4–42), and the famous 'Parable of the Good Samaritan' (Lk 10:25–37) addressed the Jews' hatred of them.

samsara (meaning 'wandering') **(B/H):** continuing process of birth and death that characterises the notion of *reincarnation*. It includes not only time spent living an earthly life, but also time 'between lives' or in other forms or places.

■ *TIP* Samsara is unsatisfying and is not a spiritual goal — the aim of the believer is to be free from samara, the cycle of birth, death and rebirth.

samskara (H): loosely translated as 'sacrament', refers to the traditional Hindu life-cycle rites.

■ There are, traditionally, 16 samskaras, but these have been reduced in modern times to cover the rituals surrounding birth ('jatakarma'), the naming ceremony ('namakarana'), initiation ('upanayana'), marriage ('vivaha') and the funeral ceremony ('antyesti samskara').

Samuel (OT): son of Elkanah and Hannah, and the last great judge of Israel.

■ He ruled Israel through a period of peace and, in his old age, was guided by God to appoint a king for Israel, Saul (1 Sam. 10:1). Later, after Saul had disobeyed God, Samuel anointed David as king (1 Sam. 16:13).

■ *TIP* An interesting and important character who often appears in Old Testament examinations. Questions tend to concentrate on the various roles Samuel plays — prophet, priest, judge and kingmaker.

Sangha (B): community of Buddhist monks and nuns, and one of the 'three jewels' ('*tisarana*') to which a Buddhist must go for 'refuge'.

■ It is supported entirely by support from laypeople, who provide all the material needs — foods, medicines and so on. By this support, laypeople may gain 'merit' ('*punna*'). The Sangha itself offers teaching and spiritual guidance to the lay community.

Sanhedrin (NT): supreme Jewish council and highest court at the time of Jesus.

■ It sat in Jerusalem and was made up of chief priests and elders, who would assemble whenever necessary for matters of religion and administration. It dealt with the religious problems of the Jewish community, collected taxes and acted as a civil court when necessary. The Sanhedrin conducted the preliminary trials of Jesus (Mk 14:53–65) and Paul (Acts 23:1–10).

S

Sant-sipahi (S): term in Sikhism meaning 'ideal Sikh'.

■ On the one hand, a Sikh should be pious and humble, devoted to the '*Nam*', like a holy person ('sant'). On the other hand, the Sikh should be courageous and prepared to fight for justice, like a soldier ('sipahi').

Satan (OT/NT/I): name given to the Devil, the fallen angel who opposes God.

■ In the Old Testament, Satan is 'the adversary' who appears in the Book of Job, where he is shown to be a heavenly being whose task it is to inform God of human weaknesses. However, in 1 Chronicles 21:1, he is depicted as a more sinister entity. In the New Testament, he tempts Jesus in the wilderness (Lk 4:1–13), is called the enemy of God (Lk 22:3) and is said to have legions of demons who may enter and tempt human beings to do evil (Lk 9:42). The Book of Revelation says that, finally, Satan will be cast into the lake of fire (Rev. 20:10–15).

In the Hebrew-Christian tradition, Satan is the supreme embodiment of evil, sometimes called the Devil.

In Islam, he is called 'Iblis' and 'al-Shaitan'. Iblis is an angel who disobeyed God by refusing to acknowledge Adam as his superior. He was expelled from Paradise. Al-Shaitan seeks to lead humanity astray with the aid of evil spirits. On Judgement Day, Ibis/Al-Shaitan and his demons will be thrown into hell-fire.

Saul (OT): first king of Israel. He came from the tribe of Benjamin and was anointed by Samuel (1 Sam. 10:1).

■ He began well, but grew proud and disobeyed God. He suffered from fits of madness and depression, and Samuel was forced to anoint David as king to succeed him. Saul initially liked David, who sang him songs to calm his moods. However, Saul soon became jealous and tried to kill him, and David was forced to flee. Saul took his own life after he was defeated in battle against the *Philistines* (1 Sam 31:4).

sceptic (P): someone who believes that it is impossible to have real knowledge of things.

scholasticism (C): theological practice used by Christian medieval scholars to work out the implications of the teachings of the Bible and the fathers of the Church.

■ The aim was to produce a consistency of approach and understanding and to reconcile contradictions. The most famous scholastic was St Thomas *Aquinas*.

scribe (from Latin term for 'writers') **(NT):** experts in the Jewish Law at the time of Christ.

■ Their task was to interpret the Law and show how it applied in everyday use. They were also experts in administration and diplomacy. The Gospels show them to be opponents of Jesus, linked to the *High Priest* and the elders (Mk 11:18).

Second Coming (also called *parousia*) **(NT):** refers to a time when, according to Christ, the '*Son of Man*' will come. It will be after a time of conflict and suffering

(Mk 13:30) and will be a time of judgement (Matt. 13:41–43) and the establishment of the *kingdom of God.*

■ Many Christians see the Second Coming as the return of Christ, and this is supported by Paul in 1 Corinthians 15 where he suggests that, when Christ returns, the dead will be raised up. In John's Gospel, Christ speaks of the time when he will return and take his disciples to the place he has prepared in his father's house (Jn 14:3). Although it is widely accepted that the 'Second Coming' refers to the return of Christ, the New Testament never actually uses the term 'the Second Coming of Christ'.

Second Vatican Council (1962–65) (C): council called by Pope John XXIII in order to examine and renew the life of the Roman Catholic Church and to bring its teaching, discipline and organisation up to date. The ultimate aim was the unity of all Christian believers.

■ The Council's deliberations resulted in considerable changes in the attitude of the Catholic Church towards other bodies, both Christian and non-Christian, and to the world in general. In addition, worship was made simpler by the use of vernacular (commonly spoken) language, and there was a new liturgy and a less authoritarian attitude within the Church.

secularism (P): system of thought and practice that rejects religion, or places it outside the realm of ordinary life.

■ For instance, it may be claimed that, in a country where religion is not seen as important, the society is a 'secular' one.

Sermon on the Mount (NT): famous discourse of Jesus recorded in Matthew 5–7. It seems to be a compilation of many of Jesus' teachings.

■ The first part consists of the nine *Beatitudes* or blessings, which highlight how, in the *kingdom of God,* many earthly values will be reversed. These are followed by a setting out of the ideals of the kingdom as opposed to life on earth — sayings about murder, adultery and relationships. After these comes a collection of teachings on *righteousness,* generosity and self-discipline and the *Lord's Prayer.*

Servant of the Lord (OT): refers to the servant featured in four passages of the Book of Isaiah known as the 'Servant Songs'.

■ The songs concern a servant who suffers greatly without deserving to, and his death is seen as the means by which the sins of the nation are taken away. Mystery surrounds the identity of the servant — was he an individual or a group, or did he represent the faithful *remnant* of Israel? The early Christians saw the Servant Songs as a prophesy concerning Christ, whose suffering and death led to forgiveness of sins. This theme was taken up by Paul in Philippians 2:6. The Servant Songs are found in Isaiah 42:1–4, 49:1–6, 50:4–9 and 52:13–53:12.

Shabbat (J): Jewish term for the Sabbath, which occurs on Saturday.

■ It is a day of complete rest to celebrate the creation of the world by God and his 'rest' on the seventh day (Gen. 2:2). It also commemorates the freeing of the Israelites from slavery in Egypt (Deut. 5:12). The Talmud lays out 39 main types of work which are forbidden on the Sabbath, in line with the requirement in the *Ten Commandments* to 'Remember the Sabbath day by keeping it holy' (Exod. 20:8–11). There are also several Shabbat rituals, including the lighting of candles before sundown on Friday evening, 'kiddush' (the sanctification of the day) said over wine on Friday evening and Saturday lunchtime, and the ceremony of separation ('havdalah') on Saturday evening.

shahada (I): profession of faith in Islam: 'There is no God but God, and Muhammad is his messenger.'
- It is an essential aspect of Muslim worship and one of the five *Pillars of Islam*.

Shekhinah (Hebrew for 'Divine Presence') **(J):** Jewish term for the immanence of God in the world.
- It refers to the closeness of God to humanity and his loving concern for all people.

Shema (Hebrew for 'Hear!') **(J):** fundamental expression of faith in Judaism.
- It comes from Deuteronomy 6:4–9, 11 and 13–21 and Numbers 15:37–41. It affirms the unity and oneness of God, the complete love with which he must be served, and the acceptance of his commandments. It then speaks of God's saving actions in history. The Shema is recited twice daily in the Jewish liturgy and by believers before retiring at night. It should also be said by those on the point of death.

Shi'ah (I): one of the two great forms of Islam (the other being *Sunni*).
- It originally referred to the partisans (Shi'ah) of 'Ali' (those who recognised Ali and his descendants as the true *Imams*) and, over the centuries, this group developed its own body of law and its own theology. Shi'is are predominant in Iran and Iraq.

Shiva (H): Hindu god (the destroyer) who completes the great triad of Hindu gods with *Brahma* the creator and *Vishnu* the preserver.
- Shiva's destruction is not evil, it is simply a stage in creation–existence–destruction and is seen as a natural event, such as death. Shiva is a yogi, meditating in the Himalayas. His wife is *Parvati*, the mother of the world, and their children are *Ganesha* and Karttikeya.
  Shiva is sometimes shown in the form of Nataraja, the King of Dancers, whose dance shows the creation, preservation and destruction of the universe and the chance of freedom and liberation from it.

sign (P): pattern or object which points to something else, but which does not participate in what it points at.
- For instance, a notice saying 'Turn right for St Mary's church' is a sign because it points to the church, but is not part of the church.
- *TIP* This concept, contrasted with the notion of '*symbol*', is important in religious language.

Sikhism (S): monotheistic religion, founded in the fifteenth century by *Guru Nanak* (1469–1539).
- Nanak tried to transcend Islam and Hinduism by creating a new religion. Sikhism emphasises devotion to God as the formless Creator who has revealed

himself to humanity. God cannot be found through religious rituals, but through meditation on the divine name of God and through hard work and sharing. The followers of Sikhism are called Sikhs.

sila (B): Buddhist term meaning 'wholesome conduct' — the basis of Buddhist ethical conduct.

■ The way of sila is to follow five precepts, or bases of training ('sikkhapada'), namely refraining from: (1) harming living creatures; (2) taking what is not given; (3) sexual misconduct; (4) false speech; (5) intoxication. The following of these precepts is an essential part of becoming a Buddhist.

sin (OT/NT/C): that which separates humanity from God. It does not always mean disobedience to God.

■ In the Old Testament, the term was used to highlight what was unacceptable to God, for example idol worshipping. When sin came into the world it was said to provoke God's anger (Gen. 3:24) and death was due to sin (Gen. 2:17). In the New Testament, it is used in a variety of ways — it can mean 'missing the mark' or falling below the standard required of God (Jn 8:46; Rom. 5:12), and a person can be said to fail to do what God requires. In essence, however, sin is seen as that which cuts humanity off from the life-giving relationship with God. Christianity teaches that everyone is infected with sin as a result of the fall of Adam (*'original sin'*) and the condition cannot be reversed by humanity — only by God's grace, given through belief and faith in the atoning death of Christ (Jn 3:3).

■ *TIP* Sin is often misunderstood. It does not mean 'doing wrongful things' like stealing. Such actions are symptoms of humanity's sinfulness, and may sometimes be called 'sins', but sin itself is part of the human condition. It may be helpful to think of sin as a kind of 'flaw' within human make-up which leads us to do wrongful actions and reject God.

situation ethics (E): ethical/religious notion which stresses the importance of acting according to the present situation, rather than relying on legalism and rules.

■ It suggests that our decisions should be primarily guided by a concern for the consequences of an action and how it will affect others, rather than by rules. In Christianity, this might be reflected in the notion of, for example, love for others and the love of God (*'agape'*). The subject is associated with Joseph Fletcher and his work ***Situation Ethics*** (1966).

Solomon (OT): son of King David and Bathsheba, who succeeded his father as King of Israel. He reigned from about 962–922 BCE.

■ He reigned through a period of peace and prosperity. Solomon fortified Jerusalem, increased the power of his army and made many international peace and trading agreements, sometimes through marriage alliances — he had 700 wives and 300 concubines. He was famous for his great wisdom in deciding complex issues. He built the first *Temple* in Jerusalem and permitted worship in local shrines, called the *'High Places'*. However, Solomon became unpopular

S

because of his lavish lifestyle and the ill-treatment of his people, whom he taxed heavily. His toleration of foreign wives and beliefs caused great controversy, and when he died the ten northern tribes rebelled against his son, Rehoboam, and the land of Israel was divided.

Solomon's story is found in 1 Kings.

Son of David (OT/NT): Messianic title, derived from the notion that the *Messiah* would be a descendant of King David.

■ It is a title that is used in the Gospels to refer to Jesus, e.g. Matthew 1:1; Mark 10:47.

Son of God (OT/NT): (1) in the Old Testament, title given to the King of Israel (Ps. 2:7) and, in its plural form, used to describe faithful Jews; (2) in the New Testament, often used to refer to Jesus, who is depicted as the Son of God to show his divine origin (Jn 1:18; Rom. 1:4).

Son of Man (OT/NT): phrase often used by Jesus himself — found in the Old Testament and *Apocrypha*.

■ It comes from the Old Testament and is a form of address used by God when speaking to the prophet Ezekiel and in Daniel 7:13. In Psalm 8:4 it is used to represent the people of Israel. Later on, in apocryphal literature, it was used to refer to a supernatural figure who would bring salvation and judgement, and this may be the way in which Jesus used it, perhaps in reference to himself.

source criticism (OT/NT/C): aspect of *biblical criticism*.

■ It looks at where biblical material actually comes from; it is most commonly used when investigating whether or not the authors, particularly of the Synoptic Gospels (Matthew, Mark, Luke), used the same or similar source material.

spiritual gifts (*charismata*, from Greek for 'gifts of grace') **(NT):** said to be endowments given by God to believers (Gal. 5:22–23). These gifts are different to each individual and are to be used for the body of Christian believers.

■ They are listed by Paul in Romans 12:6–8 and 1 Corinthians 12:8–10, 28–30 and comprise the gifts of speech, speaking in *tongues*, interpreting, service, administration, teaching, healing, prophecy, miracle-working, apostleship and leadership.

stoicism (C/P): Graeco-Roman school of philosophy which originated from Athens under Zeno of Citium, and which had a considerable influence on ideas in the Roman Empire at the time of Christ.

■ Stoicism depicts God as an all-pervading energy by which the world was made and is continually sustained. This is achieved through world reason or '*logos*', which shows itself in the order and beauty of the world. To be a Stoic means to be a good and wise person, and wisdom is said to come from living in accordance with the law of the universe which is embodied in the wisdom of God.

subjective (P): in philosophy, term describing a personal reaction.

■ In a sense, what is subjective might be true for you, but it is not necessarily experienced or provable to others. It contrasts with an objective experience, which is encountered by all or many. For instance, if you see an angel, but nobody else is there to see it with you, then seeing the angel is a subjective experience and people will have to take your word for it. However, if you look up and see the moon, and others have seen it too, then it is an objective experience — they don't have to take your word for it, they can see for themselves — this is an 'objective' experience.

Sufism (I): mystical movement in Islam. Its followers are called 'Sufis'.

■ The term 'Sufi' means 'wearer of wool', and it refers to the rough garments worn by ascetics. Sufis follow the 'Sufi path' through the stations of renunciation of the world and emphasise the importance of the spiritual gifts conferred by God as the real way to find communion with him. In this way, the ideals of self-annihilation ('fana') and the indwelling of the divine being ('hulul') may be achieved.

summum bonum (P): term used by *Kant* to mean the highest good, which comprises virtue and happiness.

Sunni (I): one of the two great forms of Islam (the other being *Shi'ah*), based upon the Sunna, a custom or code of behaviour that follows the example of the Prophet Muhammad.

■ The Sunna confirms and explains the Qur'an, and is one of the main sources of divine law ('Shari'a') recognised by Sunni Muslims.

symbol (P): pattern or object which points to an invisible spiritual reality and participates in it.

■ For example, the *Cross* in Christianity is a symbol because it points beyond itself and contains within it real meaning and significance for participants in Christianity.

■ *TIP* This concept, when contrasted with the notion of *'sign'*, is important in religious language.

synagogue (NT/J): main public institution of Judaism.

■ The first synagogues probably appeared during the time of the *Exile* in the sixth century BCE. At the time of Christ, most Jews outside Jerusalem met together at the synagogue on the *Sabbath* for a service of worship, and every synagogue had a chest, or *Ark*, in which the scrolls of the Law were kept. The synagogue also served as a school and a centre for local government and administration, as well as acting as a kind of community centre. The Gospels show Christ regularly visiting synagogues and teaching there, e.g. Luke 4:16. In Judaism, the synagogue is led by laypeople who are elected into office, and there are no priestly roles. At the centre of the synagogue is a 'bimah', or raised platform, from which the *Pentateuch* is read and where the cantor may lead the prayers. In Orthodox synagogues, women and men sit separately, but in Conservative and Reform traditions the sexes may sit together.

syncretism (OT): combining of two different religions.

■ It is an important notion in the Old Testament, for example when the people of Israel allowed their beliefs to become mixed with those of the Canaanites and other foreign cults. Such mixtures were condemned by the prophets, particularly Amos and Hosea, and syncretism played a large part in the unrest which occurred at the end of the reign of King Solomon.

synoptic problem (NT/C): question of the literary relationship between the three Synoptic Gospels (Matthew, Mark and Luke), as they seem to share quite a large amount of common material.

■ The most popular theory behind this is that: (1) Mark was the earliest Gospel and the other Gospel writers used it as a framework; (2) then the writers of Matthew and Luke used a now-missing document (called 'Q'), which contained further information; (3) then the writers of Matthew and Luke used sources of their own (called 'M' and 'L' by scholars).

tabernacle (OT/NT/J): portable sanctuary, used in Old Testament times, particularly during the Exodus, as a kind of dwelling place for God within his people.
■ It consisted of two components, the inner part being the 'Holy of Holies', where the *Ark* of the Covenant was kept. In the period of the Exodus, the structure was taken down and reassembled by the *Levites* every time the people moved on (Exod. 25:8; Num. 1:51). In Judaism today, traditional Jews dwell in a tabernacle ('sukkah'), taking with them four agricultural 'species' — a palm branch, a citrus fruit, three myrtle and two olive branches, which they shake each day to symbolise the end of the agricultural year and the start of the rainy season. These are waved during morning prayers in the *synagogue* and carried around the synagogue platform while prayers are chanted. This is not done on the *Sabbath*. On the seventh day, the species are carried around seven times. In Judaism, the Feast of Tabernacles is an autumn festival. In biblical times, the people were required to 'live in booths' (Lev. 23:41) for 7 days as a thanksgiving for the safety of the tribes when they were wandering in the desert during the Exodus. In New Testament times, the Court of Women in the *Temple* was lit for 7 days by giant candelabra, and was the context of Jesus' discourse on being the 'light of the world' (Jn 8:12). The eighth day of tabernacles is a separate festival called 'Shemini Atzeret'.

tahara (I): state of ritual purity in Islam.
■ It is required before participation in the *salat* (worship) and before touching the Qur'an and participating in other ritual acts.

Talmud (J): main text of rabbinical Judaism.
■ The Talmud is a commentary on the *Mishnah* and is divided into the 'Halakhah' (legal and ritual matters) and the 'Aggadah' (theological and ethical matters).

tefillin (J): two small black leather boxes which are worn by adult male Jews on the left arm and head during weekday morning services.
■ They contain parchments with four written passages — Exodus 13:1–10, 11–16; Deuteronomy 6:4–9, 11; 11:13–21.

teleological argument (P): also known as the 'argument from design', one of the Classical arguments for the existence of God.

■ The argument is based on the notion that by observing the working order of nature it can be inferred that the order must be a product of design and that therefore there is a God who designed it. This theory was included in *Aquinas'* 'Fifth Way' in his work ***Summa Theologica***.

Temple (OT/NT): refers to any of three buildings erected by the Jews in ancient Jerusalem. It is the central sanctuary and the permanent dwelling place of God among his people.

■ The first Temple was built by King Solomon and was rectangular with two courtyards. The inner part of the building was the 'Holy of Holies', in which the *Ark* of the Covenant was kept.

A second Temple was built by exiles returning from Babylonian captivity after the first was destroyed by Israel's enemies. This lasted for 500 years and was replaced by a spectacular Temple built by King Herod the Great.

Herod's Temple took many years to complete and was finally finished in 64 CE. It was surrounded by huge walls. It had an outer court, used for public debate and business, with a Court of Women (Mk 12:41), a Court of Israel (for men) and the Priests' Court. Inside the building, a curtain separated the 'Holy of Holies' from the rest. Only the *High Priest* could enter here, on the Day of Atonement. The Temple occupied a quarter of the entire area of the city of Jerusalem. It was destroyed by the Romans soon after the Jewish Revolt of 70 CE.

Ten Commandments (or 'Decalogue') **(OT):** law given by God to Moses on Mount Sinai in Exodus 20:2–17, seen as the foundation principles for the life of the Israelites.

■ The Ten Commandments include commandments prohibiting theft, murder, adultery and keeping the *Sabbath* day holy. They were written on stone tablets and kept in the *Ark* of the Covenant. They are seen as God's *'covenant* law' for Israel and are the terms of the covenant made between God and the Jews — they were his people; he had rescued them from their enemies and now he expected them to respond by obeying his laws.

Tertullian (c. 160–225 CE) (C): African Church father who wrote several major theological works.

■ In ***Apologeticum*** (c. 197) Tertullian attacked paganism. In ***De Praescriptone Haereticorum***, he claimed that only the true Church possessed the authority to interpret scripture. In ***De Anima***, he discussed the doctrine of the *Fall* of Man and *original sin*.

Test Act (C): Act passed in 1673 requiring all holders of office under the English Crown to receive Holy *Communion* according to the usage of the Church of England, to take Oaths of Supremacy and Allegiance to the Sovereign and to make a 'Declaration against *Transubstantiation*'.

■ The Act remained in force until 1829.

theism (C/J/I): belief that there is one God, who is a personal being, with every perfect quality (goodness, knowledge etc.), who is creator of the world and interacts with it, although existing separately from it.

t

■ This God is the only proper object of worship.

theodicy (from Greek *theos*, meaning 'God', and *dike*, meaning 'right') **(P):** theory which purports to explain the answer to the problem faced by the theist who asks: 'How can there can be an all-powerful and all-loving God when there is so much evil and suffering in the world?'

■ The answers include ideas concerning the nature of human free will and *original sin*. There are three famous theodicies — Augustinian, Iranean and Process.

Theravada (meaning 'doctrine of the elders') **(B):** type of Buddhism practised in Sri Lanka and southeast Asia. Classical Theravada says that there are three alternative goals — *Arahat, Paccekabuddha* and fully-awakened Buddha.

■ *TIP* Theravada differs from the other main type of Buddhism, *Mahayana*, because it rejects the suitability of the *Bodhisattva* role for all and does not accept the authority of the Mahayana scriptures.

Thomism (C): theological school that follows the teachings developed by St Thomas *Aquinas* (c. 1225–74) and has held an important position in the Roman Catholic Church for centuries.

■ The teachings include the view that, whilst certain truths about the nature of God can be deduced by natural reason, there are other truths which are beyond reason and can only be known by God himself revealing them.

timeless (P): existing outside time and unhindered by the limits of time.

tipitaka (meaning 'three baskets') **(B):** name given to the canonical collection of the Buddhist scriptures which are regarded as the word of the Buddha himself ('Buddhavacana').

■ The texts are extensive and are classified according to three divisions — 'vinaya' (monastic discipline), 'sutta' (discourses) and 'abhidhamma' (further teachings).

tisarana (B): Buddhist term meaning 'refuge', which usually refers to the 'three jewels' of Buddhism — namely '*Buddha*', '*dhamma*' and '*Sangha*'.

■ Going to the three jewels for refuge is regarded as an essential part of becoming a Buddhist.

■ *TIP* Going for refuge is not a once-and-for-all initiation into Buddhism, but is an important ritual and expression of faith.

tongues (also called 'glossolalia') **(NT/C):** refers to talking or singing in a language which is unknown to the speaker and is a gift of the *Holy Spirit*.

■ It stems from the Day of *Pentecost*, when the *Apostles* were filled with the Holy Spirit and spoke in tongues to the astonished crowd (Acts 2:4). In 1 Corinthians 14:6, Paul mentions the ability to speak and to understand tongues as being a spiritual gift. Tongues plays an important part in several Christian groups today, most notably in Pentecostalism and charismatic worship.

Torah (from the Hebrew term for 'teaching') **(J):** general word applied in Judaism to the divine teaching of God. It refers in particular to the first five books of the Hebrew Bible (Old Testament), called the *Pentateuch*, and is sometimes used in a wider sense to mean the whole of the Hebrew Bible, the oral teachings of Judaism and traditional Jewish Law.

t

■ The Torah is regarded as the result of the *covenant* between God and Israel. The Scroll of the Pentateuch is read publicly in the synagogue and is sometimes called the 'Book of the Torah' ('Sefer Torah').

transcendent (P): in a general sense, term meaning 'being beyond', used in the context of talking about God, who is said to be not only transcendent himself, but also to have transcended himself when he created the world.

■ In a narrower sense, the word is used to mean being beyond the limits of any possible experience. *Kant* suggested that there could be no knowledge of anything transcendent.

Transfiguration (NT): event recorded in Matthew 17:1–8, Mark 9:2–8 and Luke 9:28–36, regarded as a preview of Christ's resurrected glory.

■ It is an apparently supernatural incident in which Jesus takes three disciples, Peter, James and John, to the top of a mountain. When they reach the summit, Jesus is transfigured — that is, for a short while he takes on a heavenly appearance, where his face shines and his clothes become as white as light. The Old Testament figures of Moses and Elijah then appear and talk to him.

transubstantiation (C): doctrine whereby, in the *Eucharist* service, the bread and wine are deemed to become the 'body' and 'blood' of Christ. The properties of the bread and wine remain the same, but their 'substance' is replaced by that of Christ.

■ The doctrine was established in the Roman Catholic Church by the Fourth Lateran Council of 1215. In the *Reformation*, the notion of transubstantiation was rejected by Anglicans.

■ *TIP* As a simple way to understand this notion, transubstantiation means that, for Catholics, the bread and wine become, in some real sense, the body and blood of Christ. For Protestants, the bread and wine are seen as the body and blood of Christ only in a symbolic sense.

tribes of Israel (OT): in the Old Testament, the division of the people of Israel into 12 tribes who traced their ancestry back to 10 of the 12 sons of Jacob: Reuben, Simeon, Judah, Issachar, Zebulun, Dan, Naphtali, Gad, Asher and Benjamin. The remaining two tribes were named Manasseh and Ephraim, after the sons of Joseph.

■ The descendants of the most famous son, Joseph, were sub-divided into the tribes of Ephraim and Manasseh, whilst the descendants of Levi had a priestly function and possessed no land. After the *Exile*, the tribal distinctions became blurred and the number 12 became symbolic — hence Jesus had 12 disciples, representing the 'new' Israel.

Trinity (C): Christian doctrine, the notion of one God in Three Persons — Father, Son and *Holy Spirit.*

■ The clearest illustration of this comes in John 14:7–10, where Jesus refers to his Father who sent him, and in John 16:13–15, where Jesus talks of the coming of the Holy Spirit.
The word 'Trinity' is not used in the Bible. The concept was formulated by the Council of Nicaea in 325 CE.

unclean (OT/NT/J): in the Old Testament, the term applied to certain animals and fish that people were forbidden to eat. A complete list is given in Leviticus 11.

■ People might themselves become 'unclean' in certain circumstances, for instance if they touched a dead body (Num. 19:11) or came into contact with leprosy (Lev. 13:3).

Rules governing methods of purification from uncleanliness were carefully laid out and had to be followed. The laws concerning cleanliness were probably made to emphasise the difference between Israel as a holy nation and the rest of the world.

In the New Testament, many of these rules were challenged as being inconsistent with Christian notions of love and fellowship (Acts 10:15; Rom. 14:15).

univocal (P): having only one meaning and being unambiguous. It refers to words or phrases which are clear and straightforward.

unleavened bread (OT/J): bread made without yeast, used in Old Testament times as a cereal offering in the *Temple* (Lev. 2:4, 11).

■ It is associated with the period of the Exodus, where, according to tradition, the people of Israel had to leave Egypt so swiftly that there was not enough time to let the dough rise in the bread (Exod. 12:14–20). The Feast of Unleavened Bread took place at the beginning of harvest and is closely associated with the Feast of the *Passover*.

Upanishads (from Sanskrit, meaning 'a sitting down near [a Guru]') **(H):** portion of the Hindu texts which make up the *Veda*, and which some regard as the source of Hinduism.

■ They teach about the essential self (*atman*), which is within all living beings and remains pure and untouched through the process of *reincarnation*. One of the most famous Upanishads is the *Bhagavad Gita*.

Urim and Thummim (OT): a means by which the leaders of the Israelites believed they could obtain God's guidance (Deut. 33:8).

■ They were probably stones or pebbles which the priest would throw down on the ground in an attempt to 'understand' what God was saying from the pattern that the stones made (1 Sam. 14:41).

utilitarianism (E): ethical theory which states that an action is right if it conforms to the 'principle of utility'.

■ This theory was formulated by Jeremy *Bentham* in his work ***An Introduction to the Principles of Morals and Legislation*** (1789). He states that an action conforms to the principle of utility if its performance will produce more pleasure or happiness, or prevent more pain or unhappiness, than any alternative actions. The characteristic feature of utilitarianism is that the rightness of an action depends entirely on the value of the consequences.

Vaisheshika (H): one of the six salvation-philosophies ('*darshanas*') of Hinduism and probably originating from the work of Kanada in the second century BCE.

■ In the text 'Vaisheshika-sutra', Kanada suggests that spiritual development and liberation ('*moksha*') can be achieved by an understanding that the world is constituted from six categories ('padartha'): substance, quality, activity, commonness, particularity and unity.

varna (H): term referring to the four 'classes' or divisions which existed within Hindu society.

■ The highest class were the '*Brahmans*', followed by the '*Kshatriyas*', the 'Vaishyas' and the 'Shudras'. One of the hymns of the Rig-Veda, known as the 'Perushukta', says that the four classes were formed at the creation of the world, when the primal being, called 'Purusha' ('man'), was sacrificed. From his mouth came the Brahmans, from his arms the Kshatriyas, from his thighs the Vaishyas and from his feet the Shudras.

■ *TIP* The four classes are scriptural and should not be confused with the Hindu social order, which is called the '*caste*' system.

Veda (from Sanskrit, meaning 'knowledge') **(H):** large body of literature that is regarded by many as the source of Hinduism, which was 'heard' at the beginning of the world by inspired sages.

■ The Veda consists of four collections of ritual verses called 'mantras', the most ancient of which is the Rig-Veda ('the Veda of Hymns'). The Veda is an important aspect of Hinduism; the mantras are chanted by priests in temple ceremonies and as part of the domestic ritual. Acceptance of the authority of the Veda is what distinguishes Hindus from members of every other faith.

Vedanta (from Sanskrit, meaning 'culmination of the Veda') **(H):** one of the six salvation-philosophies ('*darshanas*') of Hinduism. The word itself refers to the *Upanishads* as being the final part of Vedic revelation.

■ The main concern of Vedanta is seeking knowledge of the divine power, and the most important text is known as the 'Brahma-sutra'.

verification (P): means by which the truth of a statement is proved.

Vienna Circle (P): group of philosophers who met in the private Saturday seminars of Moritz Schlick (1882–1936) in Vienna from 1923, and whose outlook became known as *'logical positivism'*.

■ They adopted what they called the 'verifiability principle', which was an attempt to clarify the meaning of words and statements. They believed that only two kinds of statements were meaningful: those whose 'truth' could be tested by the experience of the senses — see, hear, touch etc. — and 'analytical' statements such as mathematical proofs and tautologies or logical necessities. They said that all other statements were, in a sense, meaningless, since their truth cannot be verified — and this included many religious statements.

Vipassana (B): one of the two main types of Buddhist meditation practice.

■ It is said to be a direct experience and insight into reality, which is brought about by the practice of constant awareness of the 'four foundations' — body, feelings, state of mind and mental processes.

Virgin Birth (NT/C): in the New Testament, the Gospels of Matthew and Luke claim that Jesus was born of Mary without the intervention of a human partner — that is, he was conceived without sexual intercourse, and the pregnancy was instead instigated by the *Holy Spirit* (Matt. 1:18; Lk 1:35).

■ This is said to be in accordance with Old Testament prophecy, where Isaiah predicted a birth from a 'virgin' (Is. 7:14). In the Christian Church, it has come to signify the divine origin of Jesus.

Vishnu (H): sustainer or preservation god — one of the most important Hindu gods and a member of the principal triad, along with *Brahma* and *Shiva*.

■ He is depicted as a king whose task is to protect his land and his people. He preserves the world by becoming incarnate in the form of various *'avatars'*, in order to defeat the forces of evil. Two of his most famous incarnations are as *Rama* and *Krishna*. His consort is Lakshmi, the goddess of good fortune.

In art, Vishnu is blue in colour with the 'cakra', a flaming wheel. His animal symbol is 'Garuda', the king of the birds.

His name is mentioned in the '*Mahabharata*' and the 'Ramayana' epics.

Vulgate (C): Latin version of the Bible.

■ This was mainly the work of St Jerome (342–420 CE), and its purpose was to put an end to the differences between the various texts. The Vulgate itself was compiled in the sixth century CE, using much of Jerome's work, together with some older Latin translations.

Wali (meaning 'person near God') **(I)**: Islamic term for a holy man or saint.

▪ In popular Islam, many Muslims recognise a hierarchy of saints, and a local saint is seen as a very real figure, rather than the more remote prophets. Often people will ask for the saint to display healing power or to intercede for themselves and others. Pilgrimages are made to the tombs of the saints and festivals held to celebrate their lives.

Wittgenstein, Ludwig (1889–1951) (P): German philosopher, famous for his work on philosophy and religious language.

▪ In his work *Tractatus Logico-Philosophicus* (1922), he developed a theory which showed the limits of the use of language as a tool of philosophical investigation, and in *Philosophical Investigations* (1953) he developed the notion of 'language games', where he suggested that religious language is best understood by people who understand the context of the language game in which it is being used.

World Council of Churches (C): council set up in Amsterdam in 1948 as 'the fellowship of Churches which accept our Lord Jesus Christ as God and Saviour'.

▪ It is an organisation which began with the joining of two Christian movements called 'Life and Work' and 'Faith and Order'. It now includes most of the main Christian denominations of Eastern and Western Christianity, with the notable exception of the Roman Catholic Church, which is, nevertheless, a member of the 'Faith and Order Commission'. The World Council of Churches has often been involved in controversy and has tried to tackle many difficult issues including fighting racism and poverty, aiding refugees and providing spiritual guidance.

worship (C): giving of homage to the deity in gestures, rituals, words and conduct.

▪ It is likely that the earliest type of Christian worship was modelled on non-sacrificial Jewish worship, with the emphasis on reading the Bible, preaching, hymn-singing and prayers. The distinctive features of Christian worship have always been the *Eucharist* (also called 'Holy *Communion*', '*Mass*' or the '*Lord's Supper*') and the '*liturgy*', which is a fixed form of service, and, more especially in the Catholic Church, reference to the *sacraments*.

Xystus (C): place in Jerusalem mentioned by the ancient Jewish historian Josephus, who said that it was designed by King Herod the Great and used as a place for public assemblies.

■ It has been suggested that it was the scene of the trial of Jesus before Pontius Pilate.

Yahweh (OT/J): Hebrew proper name of the Deity.

■ In the Old Testament, the technical Hebrew name (*Tetragrammaton*) of God was YHWH or JHVH and, because of its sacred character, the Jews from 300 BCE onwards avoided uttering it when reading the scriptures, and used instead the term 'Adonai' ('Lord'). The word 'Yahweh' comes from the addition of vowels from 'Adonai' to YHWH in Hebrew manuscripts, and the expression occurs many times in the Old Testament.

yoga (H): related to the English word 'yoke', its main meaning is probably 'work' — that is, a kind of spiritual work to seek the divine.

■ In Hinduism, yoga is a system of ascetic and mystical discipline and practice which aims to enable the individual to develop full mastery of themselves, thereby overcoming individual limitations and imperfections and, ultimately, achieving union with the divine. There are several different approaches to yoga — ritual ('karma yoga'), devotional ('bhakti yoga'), intellectual ('jsana yoga') and meditational ('dhyana yoga'). Yoga can also refer to particular practices or techniques, for instance 'Hatha yoga', which emphasises the physical, and 'mantra yoga', which uses particular sounds.

yoga-darshana (H): one of six 'salvation philosophies' of classical Hinduism.

■ The yoga school is concerned with teaching about the stages of the spiritual path, the methods of practice and the forms of contemplative experience stemming from yoga. The most famous text is called the 'Yoga-sutra', which talks of two approaches to yoga. One emphasises cessation ('nirodha') of mental activities; the other emphasises the *Eightfold Path* with moral purification, personal control, meditation, yogic knowledge and final liberation ('*moksha*').

Yom Kippur (J): Jewish 'Day of *Atonement*' — a 25-hour fast-day which is the culmination of the 10 days of repentance of sins which began with the New Year ('*Rosh Hashanah*').

■ The Day of Atonement begins with a service of the annulment of religious vows ('Kol Nidrei') and ends the next day when three stars appear and the ram's horn ('shofar') is blown in the synagogue. On Yom Kippur there is no eating or drinking, no washing and no sexual relations. People dress in white to signify forgiveness of sins, and the Book of Jonah is often read.

In biblical times, this was the day on which the *High Priest* would enter the Holy of Holies in the *Temple* to offer incense. It was the custom to send a goat into the wilderness, symbolically bearing the sin of the people of Israel.

zakat (I): religious alms tax — one of the five *Pillars of Islam*.

■ It is paid on various types of possessions by fixed rates and the money is used for charitable purposes, as laid down in the Qur'an. Today, this tax on incomes is largely voluntary.

Zealots (NT/J): group within Judaism during the time of Christ, prepared to take up arms against the Romans who occupied Palestine.

■ The group may have had its beginnings in the social unrest of 6 CE, and one of Christ's disciples was referred to as Simon the Zealot (Lk 6:15). By the time of the Jewish rebellion in 66 CE, the group became known as a nationalist organisation gathered to fight the Romans. However, the Zealot movement seemed to end with the Roman destruction of the *Temple* in 70 CE and the mass suicide of many rebels at the fortress of Masada.

Zen (B): term meaning 'meditation' — name given to certain Japanese forms of yogic meditation.

Zion (or 'Sion') **(OT/C):** originally a fortified hill which David captured from the Jebusites, he made it into his capital, Jerusalem (2 Sam. 5:7).

■ The term became more specifically used to mean the Temple Mount area of the city (Ps. 2:6). Later, Zion was used to mean a sacred place and a secure mountain that cannot be moved (Ps. 125:1–2).

In Christian imagery, Zion was the name given to the heavenly Jerusalem and the city of the living God (Heb. 12:22).

Zionism (J): Jewish nationalist movement which sought to set up a Jewish state in the Holy Land of Israel.

■ The first Zionist congress was held in 1897 and led to the establishment of the World Zionist Organisation. The Zionist movement achieved its main aim when the State of Israel was founded in 1948. Since then, it has concentrated on providing financial aid to Israel, supporting Jewish immigrants and educating Jews around the world.

Zwingli, Ulrich (1484–1531) (C): Swiss reformer whose lectures and theological attacks on the doctrines of the Catholic Church led to the Swiss *Reformation*.

■ Zwingli became a priest in 1506, but he became disenchanted with the Church and wanted to reform it. In 1518 he was elected the 'People's Preacher' at the

Old Minster in Zürich. His lectures in 1519, where he attacked the doctrines of purgatory, the invocation of saints and monasticism, marked the beginning of the Swiss Reformation. In 1523 the city council, in support of Zwingli's reforms, allowed the Minster Chapter to become independent of episcopal control. In 1524 he declared that the *Eucharist* had a symbolic interpretation, and this led him into conflict with another reformer, Martin *Luther*, and, as a result, there could be no union between the different strands of Reformation thinking. Zwingli was killed in battle in 1531.

Zwinglianism (C): movement whose adherents followed the teachings of the Swiss reformer Ulrich *Zwingli*.

■ The basic tenet of Zwinglianism was the notion that the sole basis of truth was the Gospels. This led to a rejection of the authority of the Pope, the sacrifice of the *Mass*, the seasons of fasting and the celibacy of the clergy. Zwinglianism was most popular in Switzerland in the sixteenth century.